Law, Cultural Diversity, and Criminal Defense

American legal scholars have debated for some time the need for a cultural defense in criminal proceedings where minority cultural information seems pertinent to a finding of criminal responsibility in situations where a minority cultural defendant has violated a valid criminal statute. This work presents a systematic analysis of this issue. Drawing from sociological, anthropological, and philosophical materials, as well as traditional legal discussions, the authors develop a scheme that indicates when cultural factors can be used as the basis for such a defense and when they are irrelevant to a finding of criminal responsibility. The argument moves from general concerns of social justice that apply under conditions of social and cultural pluralism to practical policy recommendations for the operation of American criminal justice. It thus connects more theoretical materials with the practical concerns of jurisprudence. The justification for legal recognition of a cultural defense in American criminal law is anchored firmly in American constitutional law.

Craig L. Carr is professor emeritus of political science at the Hatfield School of Government, Portland State University. He has published several books and numerous articles in the areas of political and legal philosophy, constitutional law, and American politics. His more recent books include *Liberalism and Pluralism: The Politics of E Pluribus Unum*, and *Orwell, Politics, and Power.*

Lisa Johnson is a professor in the School of Business and Leadership at the University of Puget Sound, where she teaches courses in law and legal studies.

Cultural Diversity and Law

Around the world, most states are faced with difficult issues arising out of cultural diversity in their territories. Within the legal field, such issues span across matters of private law through to public and constitutional law. At international level too there is now considerable jurisprudence regarding ethnic, religious and cultural diversity. In addition, there are several layers of legal control – from communal and religious regulation to state and international regulation. This multiplicity of norm setting has been variously termed legal pluralism, inter-legality or inter-normativity and provides a fascinating lens for academic analysis that links up to cultural diversity in new and interesting ways. The umbrella of cultural diversity encompasses various population groups throughout the world ranging from national, ethnic, religious or indigenous groupings. This series particularly welcomes work that is of comparative interest, concerning various state jurisdictions as well as different population groups.

Series Editor:
Prakash Shah, School of Law, Queen Mary University of London, UK

Also in the series

Declarations of Interdependence
A Legal Pluralist Approach to Indigenous Rights
Kirsten Anker

State and Legal Practice in the Caucasus
Anthropological Perspectives on Law and Politics
Edited by Stéphane Voell and Iwona Kaliszewska

Muslim Families, Politics and the Law
A Legal Industry in Multicultural Britain
Ralph Grillo

Legal Pluralism in the Holy City
Competing Courts, Forum Shopping, and Institutional Dynamics in Jerusalem
Ido Shahar

The Challenge of Legal Pluralism
Local dispute settlement and the Indian-state relationship in Ecuador
Marc Simon Thomas

Access to Justice and Human Security
Cultural Contradictions in Rural South Africa
Sindiso Mnisi Weeks

The State and the Paradox of Customary Law in Africa
Edited by Olaf Zenker and Markus Virgil Hoehne

Law, Cultural Diversity, and Criminal Defense
Craig L. Carr and Lisa Johnson

For more information about this series, please visit:
https://www.routledge.com/Cultural-Diversity-and-Law/book-series/CULTDIV

Law, Cultural Diversity, and Criminal Defense

Craig L. Carr and
Lisa Johnson

Routledge
Taylor & Francis Group
LONDON AND NEW YORK

First published 2019 by Routledge

2 Park Square, Milton Park, Abingdon, Oxfordshire OX14 4RN
52 Vanderbilt Avenue, New York, NY 10017

Routledge is an imprint of the Taylor & Francis Group, an informa business

First issued in paperback 2019

British Library Cataloguing-in-Publication Data
A catalogue record for this book is available from the British Library

Library of Congress Cataloging-in-Publication Data
A catalog record for this book has been requested

ISBN: 978-1-138-58117-3 (hbk)
ISBN: 978-0-367-48124-7 (pbk)

Typeset in Galliard
by Florence Production Ltd, Stoodleigh, Devon, UK

Contents

Introduction

Some time ago criminal defense attorneys began making appeal to cultural factors as part of their defense strategy when representing individuals from minority cultures charged with some transgression of the criminal law. This approach to criminal defense was soon noticed by more academically oriented legal minds, and there emerged in the law reviews of the land a small flurry of controversy over the desirability and propriety of establishing something called the cultural (or culture) defense in American criminal jurisprudence. In the most general of terms, such an imagined defense "refers to a wide range of ways in which evidence about a defendant's cultural upbringing or practices could influence legal judgment about his guilt or responsibility" (Greenawalt, 2014, p. 153). To date, it appears that none of the 53 criminal law jurisdictions of the United States has officially adopted or endorsed a stand-alone cultural defense for members of minority cultures (Renteln, 2014, p. 177). Yet, the controversy continues.

And well it should, for some challenging and important concerns of social justice lurk beneath the veneer of legal technicality. Unfortunately, these concerns are rarely discussed or explored in the legal literature that surrounds this issue, and consequently, the debate over the propriety of a cultural defense in American criminal law remains largely, though by no means entirely, unconcerned with them. The purpose of what follows is to focus more explicitly upon these concerns and to derive from them an argument supporting the case for a cultural defense in American criminal law. As these remarks may suggest, the issue regarding legal sensitivity to cultural differences in criminal jurisprudence necessarily pushes the discourse beyond the confines of mere legal argument and into more theoretical waters—or at least this is the view to be adopted here. By way of introduction to what follows, then, it seems appropriate to say something in defense of this view.

I

There are two distinct ways to approach and address questions about the need for a cultural defense in American criminal law. First, one can suppose these questions fall exclusively within the domain of criminal jurisprudence and explore them as technical matters of criminal defense. Some defenders of such a defense argue that a defendant's cultural background may be invoked to establish a partial or complete excuse for an otherwise criminal act (Renteln, 2004; Note, 1986). Other defenders of the defense contend that cultural factors may be used to establish a justification for putatively criminal conduct (Chiu, 2006). And still others claim that cultural factors may properly be introduced at the sentencing stage of a criminal prosecution for purposes of sentence mitigation. But all these arguments remain within the context of traditional criminal defense and do not stray into more theoretical waters. Their supporters suppose only that Themis, the goddess of justice, should be permitted to peak out from behind her blindfold just enough to measure the psychological effect that cultural variables have on a defendant's decision to act as she or he did.

Similarly, some critics of the defense also regard the issue as exclusively a matter of criminal jurisprudence. Some of these question, sensibly enough, whether such a defense is really necessary and contend, or at least suggest, that the concerns of culture can be used within the context of traditional criminal defense to help sharpen understanding of the mental state of the defendant to see if it fits the requirement of the specific charge(s) she or he faces (Greenawalt, 2014; Golding, 2002). This view raises an important question about what a stand-alone cultural defense would look like in practice and why the legal concerns of the proponents of the defense discussed in the previous paragraph should justify a policy shift in the mechanics of criminal defense.

Other critics appear to want to stay within the narrow parameters of this legalistic approach, but broaden their arguments sufficiently to include consideration of what might be regarded as basic principles of the rule of law. Some insist, for example, that such a defense would violate the principle of equal treatment of the law by permitting cultural minorities to have access to a defense not available to members of the dominant culture. Others argue that such a defense would leave more vulnerable individuals (women and children in particular) within certain male-dominated cultural communities without legal support or redress. Still others contend, somewhat vaguely, that this defense would essentialize or reify culture in a manner that tends to undermine inappropriately judgments of individual responsibility (Renteln, 2004, pp. 192–194; Renteln, 2014, p. 181).

However, if we approach the issue as a technical matter of criminal jurisprudence, a cultural defense can make sense only as a strategy for defeating or diminishing findings of criminal responsibility. According to the mechanics of criminal law, this involves pressing either an excusing or a justifying argument in the event the defense acknowledges that the defendant did commit the allegedly criminal act. Since defenders of the cultural defense who approach the issue in the fashion now under discussion typically insist that cultural variables can excuse, mitigate, or justify putatively criminal conduct, it looks like they merely want to insist that cultural variables are relevant to assessing criminal responsibility. But this does appear to reduce to the view that cultural variables can fold rather neatly into existing criminal defense strategies without further need for a cultural defense (Golding, 2002). Thus one is left wondering why such a defense is needed and precisely what it would involve that distinguishes it from standard defense strategies.

The second way to approach the cultural defense controversy is to see it as an instance of the much larger political problem involving the accommodation of difference. The fact of social difference—cultural, religious, ethnic, ideological, and moral—is a familiar and disconcerting source of conflict and unrest within the annals of human history. In more philosophical terms, the fact of social difference introduces the problem of pluralism: How can a collection of disparate groups separated by deep and contentious normative difference, and also sharing a common social space, manage to live together in a secure, stable, and peaceful fashion? If this matter cannot be resolved successfully, then Charles Larmore's concern (borrowed from Matthew Arnold) that social life could become a place "where ignorant armies clash by night" might be realized (Larmore, 1996, p. 151). Needless to say, the problem of pluralism is much discussed within the disciplines of moral and political philosophy, political science and political theory, social theory, and legal theory. Scholars working within the liberal tradition of political thought have spent considerable time and effort addressing this problem. Their hope is that liberal theorizing can identify and articulate normative political principles that can serve as the basis for the peaceful coexistence of normatively distinct groups. Such principles would then introduce a political morality capable of establishing social justice within those civil arrangements that subscribe to them.

These reflections would seem to take us some distance from the cultural defense question. But viewed from the perspective of this second approach, the matter of recognizing the need for a cultural defense in criminal law may follow from, or be inconsistent with, general principles of social justice that guide policies suitable for the accommodation of normative difference. And there is some reason to suppose this view is rather plausible, for the problem addressed by defenders of the defense is a product of the fact of cultural difference. What we want to know, then, is how the fact of this difference should influence our thinking about the proper operation of criminal jurisprudence. So, regardless of outcome, moving to a more theoretical posture may enable us to identify principled grounds for a *political* argument that can help resolve questions about the propriety of a cultural defense in American criminal jurisprudence.

This general approach, though not as well traveled as the first approach, is hardly unheard of and has an important presence in the cultural defense literature. Alison Dundes Renteln (2004), whose work on the cultural defense is both insightful and extensive, has pushed in this general direction by arguing that a cultural defense is justified by virtue of a person's "right to culture" (p. 213). Unhappily, however, she says little about where this right comes from or why anyone should think such a right exists, other than to notice that it has a degree of currency in international law. And more recently, a collection of essays edited by Will Kymlicka, C. Lernestadt, and M. Matravers (2014) has discussed the subject in interdisciplinary fashion and opened the issue to more philosophical and theoretical analysis.

Further, it is not always easy to stay within the narrow confines of criminal jurisprudence and avoid sliding toward more theoretical matters. This is in evidence, for example, in the case of some of the critical objections to a cultural defense mentioned above. It is hardly sufficient to invoke a concern for equal treatment or protection of the law as a knock-down argument against the need for cultural defense, for example, without indicating what this principle means in practice and why it entails legal blindness to cultural difference. To make an argument of this sort stick, then, one must move in the direction of political theory. And a similar point holds true with regard to the argument that such a defense would leave vulnerable members of minority cultures without legal support or redress. This issue depends, in part, on how a cultural defense would be put to work in cases where culture variables matter when reflecting about a defendant's criminal responsibility. But it also depends upon whether the members of minority cultures, who might seem victimized by cultural practices, either want or feel the need for legal protection. And if critics reject this by insisting that vulnerable elements of minority populations should receive legal protection whether it is wanted or not, they will need to make a theoretical case for this sort of legal parentalism.

Finally, the claim that recourse to a cultural defense tends to reify or essentialize culture, thus undermining judgments about individual responsibility, can hardly stand on its own. It requires defense, and this necessarily takes us in the direction of social theory and social science, for at the very least we need to know something more about the notion of culture and how, if at all, cultural factors shape and influence individual conduct and personal decision-making. It would seem, then, that a comprehensive analysis of the need for, or desirability of, a cultural defense in American criminal law is going to require a more theoretical view than is available to those commentators who would prefer to stay within the confines of the first approach to the issue, and this sends us in the direction of the second approach.

II

Our objective in what follows is to engage the cultural defense controversy by pursuing the second approach noted above—as an instance of the political challenge of tolerance—by understanding it in a fashion that presents it as a problem of political thought and theory. While the controversy may have been inspired by criminal defense attorneys looking for clever ways to defeat or mitigate findings of criminal responsibility for their cultural minority clients, once it slipped into academic circles it gave birth to questions about how American law should properly treat citizens whose ways, beliefs, and practices differ in important ways from those of the dominant culture. It became, that is, an aspect of a more general problem about how the state should address social, cultural, religious, and moral difference—normative differences for short.

Thus reinterpreted and reconstructed, the question of a cultural defense is no longer an issue *for* criminal jurisprudence so much as it is an issue *about* criminal jurisprudence. What principles (or ideals) should govern the state's confrontation with diversity within its own citizenry? This is hardly a new or novel question, as we shall see, and there is already a substantial political and legal tradition to draw upon in thinking about this question as it applies to the fact of cultural variation. But it remains a politically pertinent, and theoretically important, question because the state's confrontation with difference is constantly changing—drifting and evolving—as the nature of social pluralism changes as a result of immigration, and what we shall call group mitosis.

As a theoretical problem, questions about the desirability of a cultural defense in American law can be addressed first by identifying fundamental principles of political morality—principles of social justice, in effect—that are compelling by virtue of their attractiveness to all concerned parties, and then by considering whether a cultural defense can be plausibly derived from them. This, by and large, is the method of argument to be employed here. Thus understood, what follows is best described as a work of applied political theory. When applied in this fashion, political theorizing yields practical policy proposals derived from more general political principles. In the present case, our policy proposals are legal in nature insofar as they are intended as recommendations for how criminal law should address the fact of cultural difference.

By way of foreshadowing the argument to follow, we intend to offer reasons in support of the view that cultural groups enjoy a right of cultural autonomy that entitles their members to practice their ways and adhere to their beliefs as they see fit. The proposed right of cultural autonomy establishes that intra-group activities and practices are not the business of the state. Consequently, the right of cultural autonomy should serve as a civil liberty that restricts government authority from intervening in the internal practices of minority cultures in the way that the free exercise clause of the First Amendment exempts religious practice from state scrutiny. This moves the discourse away from criminal jurisprudence and into the realm of constitutional law, and we shall argue that it is both possible and appropriate to find in the US Constitution a place to anchor the right to cultural autonomy. Moving this right to the status of a civil liberty, in turn, establishes a legal defense against state prosecutions that invade the sphere of cultural autonomy receiving constitutional protection. And this new approach constitutes, in effect, what we have in mind as a cultural defense against criminal prosecution.

But, as we shall see, it hardly follows that all manner of situations involving culture and the criminal law will fall within the constitutional parameters of a right to cultural autonomy. And this point introduces the possibility that not all situations in which a claim of culture is invoked for purposes of criminal defense will fall within the parameters of cultural autonomy. More generally, not all cases in which a claim of culture is invoked to defeat or mitigate a finding of criminal responsibility raise a similar problem. The existing legal literature on the cultural defense tends to be blind to the possibility that the concerns of culture pressed in the service of criminal defense contain important and distinguishable differences. If a right of cultural autonomy shields some culturally motivated conduct from criminal prosecution, it does not necessarily shield all such culturally motivated conduct from prosecution.

Accordingly, the universe of cases in which culture is introduced by way of criminal defense will be divided into three distinct categories as follows: 1) cases in which a claim of cultural autonomy holds against state prosecution, 2) cases in which culturally motivated criminal conduct are not shielded by a claim of cultural autonomy, and 3) cases in which cultural variables are necessary in order to understand a defendant's behavior but in which a matter of cultural autonomy does not apply. As will become apparent, we think a cultural defense based upon a right to cultural autonomy is dispositive of category 1 cases, but such a right does not shield a defendant from criminal prosecution in either category 2 or category 3 cases.

These conclusions exhaust the social policy proposals for the operation of the criminal justice system forthcoming below. It should be rather apparent, however, that an argument designed to sustain these conclusions will need to be highly interdisciplinary in nature. Perhaps ironically, the field of criminal law is arguably the least crucial of the various scholarly and professional disciplines relevant to the discussion at hand. The focus on political theory and philosophy as the primary disciplinary concern is no doubt sufficiently apparent. In addition, however, it is necessary to dabble in American constitutional law, American political history, and social theory in the process of crafting our argument. Such interdisciplinary work is common enough in political thought, but it is also a tricky business, for the further the theorist wanders from her own territory the more likely the practitioners of those disciplines into which she happens to wander are to insist that she ought to mind her own business.

To some extent this is a rather unfortunate consequence of the fact that the modern academy is a fairly disciplinarily-ossified place. But the internal complexity and sophistication of the disciplines also generates reasonable and proper concern that neophytes may do more harm than good if they try to navigate around within disciplines that they do not fully understand. Nonetheless, we propose to attempt to draw from the fields of constitutional law, American political history, and social theory—and to a lesser extent criminal law, in order to flesh out our argument. Recourse to constitutional law is necessary to move from theoretical principle to legal practice. Attention to American political history is required in order to set the historical foundations for the American struggle with the problem of pluralism. And some engagement with social theory is essential in order to develop and explicate an understanding of culture that explains its importance as an influence upon human actions.

It does not seem possible to address the question of a cultural defense effectively without attempting an interdisciplinary review. We have intimated already that raising the question of a cultural defense pushes in the direction of theoretical problems of both a political and a social nature. Thus both political and social theory are implicated by virtue of the nature of the topic, and situating theoretical discussion within a specific state setting triggers a concern for the institutional nature of the setting in question. But interdisciplinary work of this sort is valuable in spite of the risks, for it can inspire an interdisciplinary discourse that can enrich and advance the general understanding of the problem at hand. If social theorists find fault with our account of culture, or if criminologists take exception to our description of the mechanics of criminal defense, the correctives may sharpen the general understanding of the issue and open new avenues for more profitable ways to think about the prospects for a cultural defense in American criminal law.

III

While identifying a plausible place for a cultural defense in American criminal law is the primary focus of the argument to follow, it is not the only one. As applied political theory, the argument moves from general principle to specific policy proposal. But the specific nature of the question of difference posed by cultural variety also invites thinking back to more general matters and advancing a claim at home in traditional political theory. This more theoretical claim addresses a general challenge posed by the fact of pluralism: When, and to what extent, should the criminal law be used to standardize interpersonal conduct in spite of normative differences that encourage or incline some groups to behave in ways that group outsiders consider wrong or objectionable? The fact of pluralism produces a problem of toleration. And the question just posed asks the extent to which a just society should tolerate normative difference.

The general consensus, within both political philosophy and political and legal practice, is that the toleration requirement—the social obligation to tolerate normative difference—is not absolute. And while we do not wish to dispute this, we do propose to question some of the proposed limitations, both theoretical and practical, commonly placed upon the toleration requirement. As we shall see, the typical approach to mediating certain toleration questions in American law may not provide minority groups with all the protection they deserve as a matter of principle. Some limitations upon the toleration requirement are typically supported, both within political theory and legal practice, by appeal to some variation of JS Mill's famous harm principle, "the sole end for which mankind are warranted, individually or collectively, in interfering with the liberty of action of any of their number, is self-protection" (1951, p. 95). This principle is commonly understood to claim that the state is permitted to interfere coercively in the activities of citizens only in order to prevent them from doing harm to others. This, in turn, is presumed to identify a limit to the toleration requirement.

The more overtly theoretical thesis defended below challenges the propriety of this familiar limitation upon the toleration requirement. The right of group autonomy, as we shall see, requires a more uncompromising commitment to toleration. It requires us to concede that one group of people holding one set of beliefs is never justified in imposing its will or its ways on another group of people whose beliefs and practices are not just different but objectionable from the point of view of the first group. Because this presentation of the toleration requirement holds as a matter of principle, it is not to be overridden by matters of degree. The A's are not justified, according to the right of cultural autonomy, in imposing their will or their ways on the B's *no matter how intolerable* they may consider the behavior of the B's to be. As should be apparent, this view will seem quite radical to many, if not most, readers; yet the test for its acceptability involves reflecting upon how liberal one feels one should be in defending principles of civil association that justly respect normative difference (cf. Williams, 2005, pp. 128–138).

IV

The interdisciplinary nature of our argument suggests the need to offer at the outset a road map of the discussion that indicates where and when the various disciplines involved enter the picture. The first and third chapters are concerned predominantly with matters belonging to political theory and American political history. The second chapter is largely taken up with concerns of social theory. Here we work up an account of culture that explains its importance and the place it occupies in directing the course of human action. The fourth chapter moves the discussion back toward legal materials. Here the right to cultural autonomy derived in the third chapter is applied to a selection of cases—some of which have been associated with a cultural defense in the standard legal literature on the subject, as well as some additional ones. In this chapter we also introduce our threefold classification of cases distinguishable by the nature of the cultural issue they involve.

The fifth chapter attempts to find a constitutional home for the right to cultural autonomy. Because this right safeguards only intragroup cultural practices, the cultural defense supported by our constitutional argument reaches only those cases in category 1—cases involving only intragroup activity. It does not reach category 2 cases because these by definition involve inter-cultural criminal activity. And it does not reach category 3 cases because these do not involve cultural practices actually sanctioned and endorsed by the cultural community to which the defendant belongs. This chapter concludes with an extended discussion of the various legal objections brought against the acceptability of a cultural defense. Our conclusion is that none of these objections reaches or defeats our account of a cultural defense primarily because they are overly and unacceptably dismissive of the toleration requirement discussed above.

This completes the substance of our argument for a cultural defense, but there remains for review the curious outlier cases in category 3. We return to this category in the sixth chapter. While it will become apparent that these cases do not fall under the umbrella of a right to cultural autonomy because the criminal activity involved is not actually sanctioned by the cultural community in question, they do raise a question whether the right to cultural autonomy might necessitate from criminal defense something like cultural deference, i.e., deferring to the normative evaluation of the wrong-doing at issue at home in the defendant's cultural community. We also explore, in Chapter 6, the viability of the frequent use of cultural factors in criminal defense strategies. Of particular concern here is the use of cultural factors to establish a defendant's diminished capacity and thus to invoke cultural influences as an excusing condition. As we shall see, there are reasons to think this method of employing cultural variables in criminal defense is rather misguided and misleading; it does little or no justice to the way cultural concerns actually influence individual actions.

V

The analysis of the relation between law and culture to follow is limited by two basic factors. First, we are concerned with the propriety of introducing cultural factors into criminal jurisprudence only in the specific context of American criminal law; thus our remarks are only directed toward the 53 criminal law jurisdictions of the United States. By way of explanation, an affirmative case for a cultural defense in any particular legal jurisdiction must depend upon the political and legal culture that underlies the jurisdiction in question. Recognition of a cultural defense, in other words, depends upon the basic political principles—the emergent standards of social justice—forged through a state's historical experience with difference and diversity. Because these experiences will vary from place to place, independent criminal jurisdictions will need to measure the propriety of the cultural defense by appeal to their own, often unique, standards of social justice.[1]

However, this point does not mitigate the fact that there are important legal and political similarities across those states influenced by the historic liberal tradition of political discourse. Because these states share a common concern about the problem of pluralism and a common desire to establish a just resolution to the problem, the possibility of a right to cultural autonomy may resonate across the spectrum of states with liberal histories and pedigrees. Our specific focus upon the American context, then, does not mean that our remarks will have no relevance for other legal jurisdictions.

Second, our concern for the relation between law and culture is restricted to the area of criminal law alone, and we shall say little about the way cultural issues should be treated in American civil law (cf. Renteln, 2004, pp. 201–205; Shachar, 2014). If it makes sense to think that a right of cultural autonomy is a requirement of fundamental standards of social justice in America, then it seems sensible to suppose that this right might figure into civil litigation as well as criminal prosecution. While we appreciate this view, we shall not pursue or develop it here.

Note

1 For a more comprehensive discussion of the issue, see Foblets, Gaudreault-Desbiens, and Renteln 2010.

1 Law, politics, and social justice

Scholarly interest in the prospects for an independent cultural defense in American criminal law emerged as a result of an influential note published in the Harvard Law Review (Note, 1986). The author(s) of the note framed the issue as a conflict between "America's commitment to the principles of individualized justice and cultural pluralism," on one hand, and "society's interests in imposing certain common values on all of its members—interests that include maintaining order and forging bonds between its people," on the other (p. 1296). The claim pressed by the note was that the case for a cultural defense "outweighs the arguments against it," meaning, presumably, that the American commitment to individualized justice and cultural pluralism outweighs the societal interest in fostering common values throughout the land.

But this way of putting things seems confused and contradictory. If the US really does have a commitment to individualized justice and cultural pluralism—a rather grand claim—then these principles would seem to belong to the catalogue of common values that society should "impose" upon all its members. Perhaps the tension alluded to resides between individualized justice and cultural pluralism on one side of the equation and the maintenance of order and the forging of common bonds between the people on the other. But this still does not eliminate the problem, for the common bond that needs to be forged may turn out to be the general acknowledgement of and respect for the principles of individualized justice and cultural pluralism. And if these things really are acknowledged and respected throughout the citizenry, it is hard to imagine that they would pose much of a threat to social order.

Perhaps this confusion can be eliminated if we move to a somewhat higher level of generality. This, in any event, is the initial move we propose to try. The author(s) of the note is right to insist that there must be some common core of values, beliefs, ideals, norms, or whatever that bind the general citizenry together and produce a common polity. At the very least, it seems appropriate to think that being on the same side politically means something substantially grander than a shared proximity of residence. And the author also seems justified in supposing that the United States is a culturally diverse place. Few scholars even remotely familiar with American history and sociology would wish to deny that the US is populated by various cultural communities that have immigrated to the land from around the globe (cf. Higham, 1955; Fuchs, 1990; Smith, 1997).

The reality of American cultural diversity calls attention to the fact that there exists throughout the land substantial difference with regard to belief systems, social practices, religious convictions, customs, languages, group histories, and the like. If we suppose, for the moment, that this description of difference is a reasonably accurate account of the social diversity present within the borders of the United States, there is reason to wonder about the nature of the political common denominator that forges political unity out of social, ethnic, racial, and cultural difference. If the historic and well-documented presence of racism, xenophobia, and nativism in American history is also called into view, further doubts about civil unity emerge. There are those who insist upon the need for America to be a melting pot where differences of all forms integrate into the "common culture" (cf. Huntington, 1981; Huntington, 2004). But scholars of various stripes have begun to abandon the melting pot imagery because the ingredients in the pot refuse to melt.

This introduces the sociological fact of normative difference, and with the acceptance of difference, the problem of pluralism emerges. How is it possible to establish political unity amidst such substantial social, cultural, religious, and ethnic difference? This is, and has been, a central challenge of civil association both in the US and across the planet at least since the modern system of states was established in Europe with the Peace of Westphalia in 1648. As an intellectual challenge, it has been a subject of conversation from Aristotle's *Politics* to the present day, and as a practical political challenge it has been with us at least as long as political leaders began to understand that political order and stability are better achieved by pursuing and promoting shared standards of justice than by the force of arms.

The theoretical and practical challenges produced by the problem of pluralism come together when we stop to ask about the standards of justice that are, or ideally should be, shared by all the citizenry, standards that society should cultivate in the hearts and minds of its members. The standards to which we refer qualify as standards of justice because they involve the articulation of principles, acceptable to all citizens, that enable *political* unity to emerge from the fact of *societal* difference. This is the vision of justice that stands behind the American motto of *e pluribus unum.* Without asking at this point what these imagined principles are, it is important to hypothesize their existence, for this is what assures us that the US is a basically just state rather than a state where the strong rule the weak by force and intimidation.

If we move forward from this heightened level of theoretical generality, it might seem appropriate to ask if something like a cultural defense in American criminal law is consistent with, or mandated by, these formative political principles—however we might elect to formulate them. Framed in this fashion, the issue raised by consideration of a cultural defense in American criminal jurisprudence no longer displays any tension between principled commitments to individualized justice and the common values of the land, as the Harvard Law Review note would have it. Instead, the propriety of such a defense depends upon whether the formative principles of social justice present in the US support, mandate or require it.

This introduces the method we will employ to consider the desirability of a cultural defense in American criminal law. It might seem that the place to begin is with a theoretical inquiry into the basic principles of social justice that forge American political unity. But the matter is not quite this simple. Disparate historical and theoretical factors complicate matters significantly. Some of these factors push in the direction of the toleration of normative difference, but others counsel in favor of greater or expanded cultural (and not just political) homogeneity and social integration.

The purpose of this chapter is to survey these various historical and sociological factors in order to set the stage for a discussion of controlling principles of social justice, which we shall undertake in the third chapter. We are primarily concerned here with the historical and legal aspects of the American experience with normative difference. The story we are about to tell in this chapter identifies in American political and legal history some limited interest in tolerating certain forms of difference and some uncertain boundaries to the extent of the toleration present in American law. This does not take us back to the tension between individualized justice versus the common values of the land (whatever these might be) that concerned the author(s) of the *Harvard Law Review* note. Instead, the discussion in this chapter is intended to introduce a somewhat different tension between an appreciation of the importance of toleration in dealing with the problem of pluralism, on one hand, and the refusal to practice toleration when normative difference seems intolerable to dominant sentiments, on the other. Before it is possible to assess the need for a cultural defense, this tension needs some form of principled resolution. But our proposed resolution will need to wait until chapter three.

Déjà vu all over again

Social pluralism of some sort has been a prominent feature of American life from the arrivals of the Puritans in New England onward. It should hardly surprise, then, if the issues raised by the introduction of cultural variables into the courtroom have a familiar ring to them. Arguably, the first instance of the divisive nature of social difference amongst European settlers upon the shores of North America, and the first appearance of something like a cultural defense in an American court of law, occurred in Massachusetts Bay in the mid-1630s. The religious disagreement that resulted from the fragmentation of Christianity in Europe quickly found its way to the fledgling settlements of New England where the Puritan orthodoxy of Massachusetts Bay put into practice the venerable tradition of religious persecution that it left Europe to escape. The names of the leaders of early religious diversity in this "new" England are familiar enough to students of American history: Anne Hutchinson, Samuel Gorton, George Fox, and of course Roger Williams—to name but a few of the most prominent dissidents of the day (cf. Zakai, 1991, p. 135).

Of these early rebels, Roger Williams is perhaps the most interesting and, for present purposes, the most important. Williams brought with him to Massachusetts Bay from his native England certain religious convictions considered misguided and dangerous by the elders of the church in Boston. He was put on trial for his open espousal of what church leaders considered dangerous beliefs and famously banished from the Colony (Rosenmeier, 1968). Escaping the clutches of the elders of Boston, who would have shipped him back to England, Williams and a few hearty followers fled to the shores of the Seekonk River and established what would soon become Providence, Rhode Island and a colony dedicated to what Williams called "soul freedom"—liberty of conscience by another name (Brockunier, 1940, pp. 56–66). Williams's new colony was committed to the practice of religious liberty; it was not the proper business of the civil government to regulate religious belief or to impose religious views on the general citizenry.

This apparently liberal view of church/state relations inclined later historians to consider Williams to be America's first liberal democrat (cf. Bancroft, 1843; Parrington, 1927), but this bit of hyperbole is now generally dismissed by more contemporary historians who regard Williams as a most devout Puritan rather than a secular political thinker (Moore, 1963). Williams reached his conclusions about the importance of soul freedom from his own theological and doctrinal convictions; for him, the separation of church and state was a theological, and not a political, requirement. As such, only those who shared Williams's theological viewpoints could also embrace the separation of church and state, and this is some distance from the contemporary liberal idea that the separation of church and state is a prior political commitment that holds, or should hold, regardless of one's religious beliefs.

At the trial that resulted in a verdict of banishment, Williams invoked his notion of soul freedom to argue that secular authority should not demand compliance with those elements of the Decalogue that address a person's relation with God. Because this was his religious belief (rather than a political conviction), Williams was in effect arguing that he and his followers should be permitted to live by their own religious convictions and practice their own theological ways free from state impositions to the contrary. This, as we shall see, can be regarded as a form of a cultural defense; it amounted to a plea on Williams's part for the Bay to tolerate religious difference. Needless to say, the saints of the Bay summarily rejected this argument. In his famous and protracted exchange with Williams that followed the trial and banishment, John Cotton defended the position of the Bay with a familiar argument. Satan will entice the flock of religious followers away from devotion to God and lead them into a life of sin unless the flock accepts the guidance and religious wisdom of the Puritan elders. The familiarity of this argument becomes evident when we appreciate its paternalism: The religious leadership of the saints is essential to protect the flock against the greatest of all possible harms—estrangement from God.

Williams lost his battle with the saints of the Bay, but there is a sense in which he eventually worn the larger war. His concern for soul freedom was eventually transformed from a religious view into a political conviction generally honored throughout the land. The actual story of this transformation is no doubt a saga of religious fear (on the part of those who worried they might hold, or come to hold, views that were in the minority) coupled with political expediency, rather than a tale about a principled epiphany that swept across the new nation. But the road to standards of social justice is almost always paved with fears and expediency of this sort. Though it may be a sad commentary on the human condition, political struggle, typified by conflict and compromise, is a considerably more effective source of insight into acceptable standards of political morality than philosophical argument and reflection. But the historical process by which shared standards of social justice emerge within a particular political setting—the path the citizens of a state traverse in the process of forging a political morality capable of galvanizing all elements of the population into a common polity—probably matters less than the end result.

In the American context, early efforts to accommodate religious difference were shaped by the now clearly liberal conviction that an official political stance of liberality (freedom from bias or prejudice) should be adopted by the new federal government. This commitment was considered significant enough to be built into the fabric of the formative document of American law, the federal Constitution. Thus, with ratification of the First Amendment in 1791, Congress was denied the authority to establish a religion and prohibited from interfering with the free exercise of religion. The political and theological atmosphere had changed significantly in the one 155 years since Roger Williams was banished from Massachusetts Bay for advocating (among other things) the need for soul freedom. At least on parchment, the United States had become a substantially more liberal place, even if many of the states that still had established religions had not.

We shall return time and again to the Williams saga, for there is reason to emphasize the leitmotif of struggle than surrounds group efforts to achieve inclusion within American social life in spite of the normative differences that might distinguish these groups from the dominant culture of the land. At the moment, however, we want to suggest that the Williams story, coupled with the emergence of religious freedom as a civil liberty, is fairly typical of the struggle for inclusion that typifies the politics of pluralism. In the US, this struggle is undertaken as both a political and a legal challenge. We mean by this that the politics of inclusion typically plays itself out in legal form.

The ideals of freedom and equality built into key amendments to the Constitution are adapted to meet the challenges at hand, and if perchance the Constitutional weaponry necessary for the promotion of social justice is not there, there is a good chance it will be added to the document, as it was in the case of the civil war amendments. Sometimes there is push-back, of course, as in the case of the Equal Rights Amendment (ERA), but this ordinarily happens when there is reason to think sufficient constitutional weaponry is already in place to support legal standards of inclusion. Perhaps, then, it is not an overly glaring generalization to say (with law school professors and grade school teachers across the land) that law, and the ideal of the rule of law, are fundamental to the way a general sense of social justice is formed, articulated, and promulgated within American political culture.

It might seem strange, then, to suggest, as the Harvard Law Review note does, that there is a tension of sorts between the fact of cultural pluralism and a uniform system of law in the US, and this strangeness should now be apparent. If the brief telling of the saga of religious difference above is a proper guide, it seems safe to say that law in America both recognizes and protects difference. This is not an indication that the law treats some groups differently than it treats others, or that some groups are above or immune from the law. Instead, it is an indication that a common standard of social justice, prescribed and promoted through the institution of law, must allow different groups to live by those ways and practice those beliefs that matter to them. This, in turn, is perhaps the most succinct practical account possible of what Americans mean when they claim to live in a "land of the free."

The idea of the rule of law holds fundamentally that no one is above the law (Waldron, 2002, p. 17). Everyone is subject to the same legal standards, including those individuals who happen to be the source of the law. But a rule of law that is capable of accommodating social pluralism must do two things: first, it must make certain that everyone honors its ends and ideals, and second, it must be sufficiently flexible to make sure that the commitment to honor difference is not compromised by otherwise reasonable legislative requirements (or specific statutes having the status of law). For some reason, elements of the population in the dawn of the twentieth century thought it wise to prohibit the use of intoxicating spirits, and for some reason, they managed to carry the day. Yet the use of sacramental wine was, and is, an important part of the religious practices of both Jewish and Catholic communities. Should a state committed to toleration of religious difference, but that has also decided that the use of alcoholic beverages is objectionable, allow or prohibit the use of sacramental wine for these groups?

We know, of course, that these communities were exempted from the strictures of the Volstead Act, and justly so. The wishes, concerns, fears, beliefs, and/or convictions of some group, whether or not it qualifies as a majority of the population, should not be imposed upon others in a way that compromises their ability to worship as they think proper. Motive does not matter here; no matter how sensible or benign the point behind such an imposition upon the religious practices of another might be, one group of people cannot tell another group of people what they can and cannot do when it comes to worshiping their deity. This is the character of the religious toleration inspired by Williams and safeguarded by the First Amendment. And it does not produce a dual standard of law, for the requirement of law is controlled by the single standard of the free exercise of religion ensconced in the fundamental law of the land. A common standard of law that applies equally and with equal force to all people, accommodates and protects religious difference and immunizes this difference from the ordinary actions of legislatures by disempowering the state from using the vehicle of law to invade their protected sphere of liberty.

The relevance of the emergence of religious toleration in the US for the question how to (or whether to) accommodate cultural diversity in American criminal jurisprudence should be reasonably apparent. If religious toleration is an appropriate standard of social justice that helps define political freedom in the US, might it not make sense to consider cultural accommodation in a similar light and suppose that Americans should also tolerate cultural difference by honoring and respecting the autonomy of the diverse cultural communities present in the body politic? It makes sense to tolerate religious difference because religion matters greatly to people. This is why we think that the forceful imposition of religious beliefs on some group that believes differently is oppressive, even if the religious views of the group imposed upon differ substantially from our own.

If culture also matters greatly to people, then the case of religious liberty would seem to represent a powerful precedent for thinking about how the US should approach the issue of cultural difference. This merely follows the tradition of inclusion in the US, a tradition that indicates how the country manages the problem of pluralism. Here political principle receives legal expression, and social inclusion is realized through the legal articulation and enforcement of the expectations of justice. This, in any event, is illustrative of the argument for the legal recognition of a cultural defense to follow.

Law and social homogeneity

"But wait!" as the familiar television advertisement goes, "there's more." If the previous section sketches the view that social justice in the US is typically formulated and endorsed through legal, especially constitutional, standards, it would seem to be a reasonably simple extension of the argument to defend the authority of law—thus establishing the authority of the legal system as the driving force behind the promotion of the ideals of justice. But it turns out that things are not quite so simple, because when we consider the authority of law—which we propose to do in this section—we find that this authority is connected in disturbing ways with a substantial degree of homogeneity. If, however, law derives its authority from the legal defense and enforcement of customary norms shared throughout society, it would seem hard-pressed to manage the problem of pluralism in the fashion suggested above.

It seems necessary, then, to say a bit more about the connection between law and justice in American politics. The institution of law operates in various and occasionally conflicting ways within the socio-political structure of society. For some, the emergence of the rule of law is a noble thing and law itself is esteemed as the very *sine qua non* of a just social order (cf. Fuller, 1964). For others—Marxists in particular—law is a vehicle of control and repression, a hegemonic device that enables the wealthy and empowered few to dominate and oppress the remainder of the population. For still others—let's call them legal positivists—law is merely law and its moral critique stands independent of its existence as a particular sort of social institution.

Perhaps each of these camps would agree, however, to the terribly general, but also rather significant assertion that law *claims* to be special. The very notion of social life implies the presence of rules that organize, cohere, structure, and direct the activities and interactions of some collection of persons (Giddens, 1984, pp. 16–20; Searle, 1995, pp. 141–147). Sometimes rules sink deep into the fabric of our being. Social life seems inconceivable without shared language, for example, but as Wittgenstein emphasized, speaking and understanding a language involves "operating a calculus according to definite rules" (1958, p. 38:e). At other times rules outline an activity in which we may or may not elect to participate. No one needs to play tennis, for example, but if one chooses to do so, one must follow the rules of the game; otherwise one is just batting a ball about with a racquet. In either case, however, to *do* something involves following a rule.

Rules both create possibilities and direct action. As Searle observed, "[Y]ou cannot desire to make a lot of money, get married, or become president of the United States unless there are the institutions of money, marriage, and the United States presidency" (2010, pp. 123–124). People are able to marry only if their social world possesses the institution of marriage, and if they choose to marry, they must follow the rules that establish what it means to marry someone. Following Anthony Giddens, we shall suppose that social institutions are identifiable by virtue of the fact that they are "more enduring features [or social practices] of social life" (1984, p. 24). These institutions (or perhaps it is more accurate to say "institutionalized social practices") organize and direct social life within some identifiable social order (Schatzki, 2002, pp. 96–102). They routinize life for the people among whom they operate and who operate through and by means of them. An orderly, coherent social condition is difficult to imagine without them.

Law, of course, is one of the more obvious examples of what we are calling a social institution. But religious and political structures also exemplify social institutions that serve to order and cohere the social relations of various peoples—institutions linked closely to the customs and traditions of these peoples. This suggests that law is one of (possibly) several distinct social institutions that work together to promote and sustain social order. Why then should law *claim* to be special?

The claim that law is special amounts to the proposal that law has and enjoys an authority that is different from, and superior to, all other social institutions present in some ordered social condition—special, that is, within the "basic structure, organization, or layout of social life" in some discernible jurisdictional context (Schatzki, 2002, p. 3). Law is a system of rules that trumps all other systems of rules in society—or at least this is what the *claim* that law is special amounts to (cf. Raz, 1979). There are, needless to say, many social institutions, both formal and informal, that contribute to social order—here things such as the rules of morality, etiquette, religion, custom, tradition, and the like come readily to mind. This, in any event, seems to be the empirical point behind the legal pluralism movement that notices the presence of diverse authoritative rule-based institutions in a "social field" and then concludes that "legal pluralism is a universal feature of social organization" (Griffiths, 1986, p. 38).

The legal pluralists are no doubt right to notice that most contemporary societies are composed of a diversity of authoritative social institutions, each of which contributes to social order in its own way. But this insight must still come to grips with the claim that law is special. This claim amounts to the view that the authority of law is superior to whatever authority these other institutions have within the social milieu. If law is special in this way, then legal rules trump the rules of all other social institutions (and practices), and in the event of a conflict between the rules of these institutions and a legal rule, social members are expected, and are presumed to understand that they are expected, to obey or follow the legal rule. This claim of superiority, of course, has long been debated and contested within various communities where the rule of law has a clear presence—witness, for example, the enduring dilemma Sophocles posed in his *Antigone* (cf. Berman, 1983, pp. 259–264).

This claim of superior authority is connected historically to the evolutionary process by which the modern state became recognized as sovereign, both within its own borders and without (cf. Berman, 1983; Elshtain, 2008). While other systems of legal order may exist within a state (for example, Canon Law or Talmudic Law), the realization of state sovereignty means that the authority of secular law trumps any jurisdictional claim of these systems in the event of a jurisdictional conflict with secular law. Although legal theorists—and particularly those belonging to the positivist tradition—are disinclined to emphasize an understanding of law that presents this institution as a dimension of the political structure of the state, they must make this connection explicit if they are to account for the authority of law, or endorse some version of natural law argument.

But natural law arguments are hard-pressed to explain effectively the authority of law because they link this authority too tightly to moral or theological concerns. As Aquinas, following Augustine, pointed out, "an unjust law is no law at all" tends to undermine rather than secure and explain the authority of law. As secular sovereign's coalesced and solidified their political power, it became rather silly to insist that a "command of the sovereign" considered unjust was not really law. Hard-headed legal positivists, such as John Austin, considered this foolish; unjust laws for Austin were most certainly laws, even if they were unjust. But if we endorse an Austinian view of law, we still cannot produce a viable defense of the authority of law. If might doesn't make right, then sovereign might doesn't either, and with this a claim of legal authority collapses.

Perhaps the most exceptional attempt to defend a version of legal positivism and also account for the authority of law is presented in HLA Hart's *The Concept of Law* (1961; see also Raz, 1979, pp. 3–33). Hart considers the development of a legal system to involve the evolution of a simple regime of customary practice toward a formalized system for the recognition, adjudication, and change of the "primary rules of obligation" that belong to customary practice (1961, pp. 92–93). According to Hart's sociological exercise, in pre-legal social conditions interpersonal relationships are governed by customary rules that are presumed or understood to have obligatory force by the members of the social milieu in which they operate. The introduction of secondary rules of recognition, adjudication, and change arise when a simple society becomes sufficiently large and complex to negate the effective management of social life by reliance upon the primary rules of obligation alone.

The secondary rule of recognition plays a special role in Hart's theory, for it enables those subject to the primary rules of obligation to identify an authoritative list of the rules that now obligate as a matter of law. This produces an obvious shift in the basis of the authority of the rules. If these rules once had authority because it was once the custom to think they identified the right thing to do or not do, they now derive their authority from the fact that they are identified as obligatory by the rule of recognition. This is because the rule of recognition is acknowledged and accepted as a source of the authority of the legal process it helps introduce. The rules of change permit legal authorities to alter or amend existing primary rules, add new ones, and remove old ones from the list of obligatory rules, and these changes also qualify as authoritative because they are done under the aegis of the rule of recognition. New primary rules do not necessarily merely codify existing customary practices, for example, but they do create new legal obligations because they must be considered authoritative. This is the natural consequence of recognizing the secondary rule of recognition as authoritative (Hart, 1961, p. 196).

This looks something like a consent theory of political authority where the authority of the government depends upon the consent (or recognition) of the governed. But the consent Hart relies upon is merely imagined or hypothesized, and one might plausibly wonder whether things move too fast at this point in the argument. It seems sensible to suppose that the members of a social system that has become complex enough to destabilize the reliance upon customary practice to sustain social order would be willing to embrace the legal mechanisms that Hart imagines as a solid strategy for securing this much-needed order. But Hart initially imagines a social system that seems quite homogeneous—a simple and apparently isolated social setting where customary rules and traditions sustain the social order. This makes the general acceptance of and agreement upon the primary rules of obligation believable enough and altogether understandable. But with increased size and growing complexity, the initial homogeneity Hart imagines would naturally seem to decay; as societies grow, they tend toward greater pluralism—consider again the fragmentation of Puritan orthodoxy in New England (Giddens, 1984, pp. 244–251).

If we remain for a moment with Hart's reliance upon the homogeneity of simple pre-legal societies, the conservative features of his argument become apparent. The legal system Hart imagines replaces customary practice as a way of integrating social norms into new elements of the population and securing compliance with these norms across the general population. The law's claim to authority, moreover, establishes this institution as the primary social mechanism for the maintenance of order and the propagation of the norms (Hart's primary rules) regulating and controlling interpersonal association. This conserves the resultant socio-legal status quo and moderates whatever pressures might emerge through time that would encourage social change. Other social forces or institutions that might serve a similar, or perhaps competing, integrative function are concurrently displaced and their influence over elements of the population diminished (Diamond, 1971; Giddens, 1984, p. 232). By extension, then, Hart's account of law seems to put in place an institution with a strong homogenizing influence on the social space within which it has authority.

It seems best to admit that law does have this affect in many places, including the United States. Nor should we take this to be a bad thing; instead, it enables law to perform an important and much needed normalizing and integrating function in society. But with this comes certain problems when the problem of pluralism is again brought into view. The fact of normative difference sits awkwardly beside the normalizing or homogenizing force of law. This is not a matter of logical contradiction, and we shall discuss shortly a way of realizing a reconciliation between law as a homogenizing force and law as an instrument of social justice within pluralist social environments. At the moment, however, there is reason to pay some attention to the challenges the normalizing force of law poses for the just resolution of the problem of pluralism.

The normalizing function of law may be invoked when immigrant communities bring with them cultural practices that stray too far from beliefs and practices of the dominant culture. (By "dominant culture" we mean simply to call attention to the fact that certain pervasive social practices, and the norms that drive them, are considered legitimate, proper, governing, or mandatory throughout the population that subscribes to them. The moral and/or social force these practices are understood to have is also expressed through, enforced by, and defended within the institution of law. While the population subscribing to these legally expressed and socially acknowledged practices need not be a majority of the entire citizenry (though it probably is), it does dominate the social centers of power and authority (e.g., political, legal, and perhaps religious institutions) operative within the state.) In the event immigrant groups bring with them practices considered deviant and intolerable according to the sympathies of the dominant culture, the force of law may be brought against these groups to prohibit and sanction their continued operation.

Arguments crafted to justify this application of law often involve claims about the need for immigrant groups to respect American ways and integrate into the general (i.e., dominant) population, or appeal to the so-called "When in Rome" argument. There is very little difference between these two arguments, of course, except perhaps that the first anticipates that new immigrant groups should integrate because this is what others have done—this is the expected tradition. This claim, however, is generally—though certainly not entirely—false (cf. Walzer, 1996). Immigrant integration into mainstream culture varies, but few groups seem to integrate entirely into the mainstream.

The second argument is more normative in nature. It is often presented as holding: (1) This is how we do things here, and (2) therefore, this is how you should do them also. But this is really no argument at all since the normative claim in (2) hardly follows from the descriptive assertion in (1). To make the argument work, it is necessary to insert something like the following premise: (1*) The way we do things here is the right way to do them. Now the argument works, but it is no longer a "When in Rome" argument. This is because fact of place no longer drives the argument; instead the claim of normative infallibility drives it.

We now have before us two distinct social functions that the institution of law is expected to perform. On one hand, we look to law to instantiate and promote shared standards of social justice. These are standards considered authoritative because they are acknowledged as necessary in order to domesticate normative difference and resolve the problem of pluralism. On the other hand, we also expect law to perform a normalizing function that slows and moderates the forces driving social change, and defends and polices social norms and practices that matter (and often greatly) to the dominant culture. While this does not produce a logical contradiction—the two views are in principle reconcilable—it does generate political tension and possible conflict. Should immigrant groups, or groups whose ways have come to conflict with the norms of the dominant culture, be tolerated as a requirement of justice, or should their ways legally be prohibited as a matter of (presumed) moral right?

The great American compromise

Resolving the cultural defense issue depends upon the propriety of the answer that is put to this question. If a suitable answer could be found within the confines of American law or politics, a solution to the cultural defense issue would most likely follow as a matter of course. We do not think, however, that such an answer can be found by searching the legal story that surrounds the American confrontation with pluralism. Instead, this story exemplifies a strategy of finessing this question that we call the great American compromise. The purpose of this section is to illustrate and defend this view by exploring the salient case law. The inability of the great American compromise to put a satisfactory answer to the question posed above will then necessitate a more theoretical confrontation with the problem the question introduces. We will return to this matter in Chapter 3.

Perhaps predictably, conceptions of how best to manage the tension that arises between the two legal functions identified above often depend upon the eye of the beholder. To illustrate, consider some religious or cultural practices held to be deeply objectionable from the moral point of view generally held by the majority of Americans. Here things like polygamy, human sacrifice, honor killings, faith healing, and female circumcision come readily to mind. It seems fair to say that the prevailing public opinion in the US is that these things should not be tolerated; they are simply too offensive according to contemporary moral sensitivities. Thus they fall into the realm of the intolerable (Warnock, 1987). When this judgment prevails, the scales of justice tip toward the normalizing function of law. In such cases, a belief in moral right frequently inclines the dominant culture to impose with a clear conscience its shared will on vulnerable minorities. This is hardly sufficient to appease the consciences of those minority groups who are imposed upon, of course, and if those groups are sufficiently strong politically, the fight is on and the problem of pluralism remains with us.

This is aptly illustrated once again by the fate of Roger Williams in Massachusetts Bay. Williams and the saints of the Bay differed on key theological matters over which there could be neither acquiescence nor compromise by either party. And the differences mattered greatly to all concerned. The only effective resolution to the conflict was separation, and fortunately for Williams and his followers, physical separation was possible. But physical separation only delayed slightly the need for colonial Americans to come to grips with the fact of religious difference. Historically, the issue of religious difference was finally addressed by recourse to religious toleration, and this took assertions of religious truth off the table as a way to settle religious conflict that ends up in a court of law . . . sort of!

The hesitation that ends the previous paragraph is intended to indicate that the matter of religious difference is not as easily remedied as the principled appeal to religious toleration would make it appear. If we agree with Williams (albeit for political rather than religious reasons) that it is wrong for government to meddle in the religious affairs of citizens, we would seem to be required, as a matter of logical consistency, to reach a similar conclusion when faced today with religious practices that we find deeply repugnant—such as, say, polygamy, human sacrifice, and faith healing. But even a quick glance, like the one to follow, at the constitutional history of religious freedom in the US demonstrates that this has not been the prevailing conclusion.

Perhaps nowhere in American constitutional law is the problem of pluralism more prominent than in free exercise litigation. The first prominent field of litigation that placed free exercise claims against social norms valued by the dominant culture involves the Mormon polygamy cases of the late-nineteenth century: *Reynolds v. US* (1879) and *Davis v. Beason* (1890). In *Reynolds*, the Supreme Court dismissed a Mormon claim that the free exercise clause protected their religious practice of polygamy on the grounds that the clause absolutely protected religious belief but did not also absolutely protect religiously motivated action from state censure. The Mormon community, throughout much of the latter part of the nineteenth century, was publicly and politically presented as a moral menace to society, and the federal Congress, which was heavily influenced by this viewpoint, passed an anti-polygamy statute aimed directly at the Mormon practice. The Court upheld the statute on the ground that religious practices that threaten the public interest do not enjoy free exercise protection. It was merely presumed, of course, that Mormon polygamy threatened the public interest, perhaps by eroding the spirit of monogamy and endangering the sanctity of the traditional American family, and this mere presumption was sufficient to persuade the Court that a putatively criminal activity did not warrant constitutional protection simply because it was associated with religious belief.

The Court would echo these sentiments 11 years later in *Davis*. In this case, the Territory of Idaho had enacted a statute that denied the franchise to members of groups who practiced or believed in the practice of plural marriage. Once again, the statute was directly aimed at Mormons who were moving into the Idaho territory and who were perceived to pose a political threat to the non-Mormon population currently in the Territory. In upholding the statute, the Court again insisted that the free exercise clause protects belief but not conduct, and the Court declared that polygamy qualifies as conduct, even though the statute included those who merely believed in polygamy, or belonged to a group that advocated such a belief, but did not in fact practice polygamy. In language immediately reminiscent of *Reynolds*, Justice Field argued that "crime is not the less odious because sanctioned by what any particular sect may designate as religion" (p. 345).

Justice Field's aggressive rhetoric hints at the low esteem in which the Mormon community was held by the "dominant religious culture" and the statute at issue in the case is itself sufficient to attest to the manner in which the Mormons were demonized in the Idaho territory and throughout the land more generally. But Field's remarks are also quite beside the point. While it might be true that the odious nature of polygamy, as judged by the majority of citizens holding different religious or moral views about marriage (here the "dominant religious culture"), is not lessened simply because it belongs to the religious practices of some group, this is hardly the issue at hand. The issue, rather, is whether the free exercise clause protects religious practices, no matter how odious they may seem to those who believe differently.

Civil liberties, such as the free exercise of religion, always protect minorities against majorities. Majorities have no need for such protection in democratic societies; here the ballot box is their defense against an abuse of political power. Minorities, however, face the problem of majority tyranny, a problem that emerges, thanks to the problem of pluralism, when democracy meets difference. If the free exercise clause does not protect religious practices considered odious by the majority of the citizenry, one wonders what it is supposed to protect. Religious practices not considered odious are in no need of such protection because the majority will not be moved to insist upon legislation limiting or prohibiting practices its number views with indifference.

In the Mormon polygamy cases, then, the normalizing function of law prevailed over the function of promoting social justice. If the Mormon community actually posed a serious threat to the moral convictions of the monogamous Christians of the land, this approach might be warranted, but a less impassioned appraisal of the issue suggests that the legal system served instead as the spear with which the dominant majority struck at a despised minority. The Mormon community displayed a difference that was viewed as odious by the general public. Field was no doubt right about this, and thus public intolerance inspired legal intolerance of the Mormon practice of polygamy.

Ironically, there was little practical need for the Court to defend the dominant religious and cultural belief in monogamy, for this was hardly endangered, but there was reason for the Court to take seriously the problem of difference that these cases introduced. If the legal system is merely a defender of the moral beliefs of the dominant normative majority, then minorities—which are different by definition—will find little relief from the tyranny of the majority. And if this really is the case, there is also little need for any constitutional posturing about the free exercise of religion. Roger Williams's soul freedom would be available only to those whose souls fell sufficiently in line with the souls of the dominant majority as not to be offensive to the latter. This is no great advance in freedom beyond what Williams experienced in the Bay.

The Mormon polygamy cases illustrate how legal contradiction has slipped into American constitutional law and taken the form of the great American compromise. Granted, polygamy is morally repugnant to many, perhaps with good reason, and, granted, the Mormons were held in low moral esteem in these early days of the republic, but even if we grant these things, the issues raised by these cases are not settled. The polygamy cases raise some tough questions about whether a just society should tolerate religious difference without regard to normative objections from the dominant culture. The normalizing function of law would support rejecting Mormon free exercise claims on the grounds that the practice of polygamy is properly and rightfully wrong and repugnant from some morally compelling viewpoint. That is, moral principle, not legal principle, is dispositive of the case. Polygamy is not to be tolerated because it is morally wrong, and accordingly, toleration reaches only social practices and activities that are not morally wrong.

We leave the qualifier, "morally wrong *according to the beliefs of the dominant culture*," out of the last sentence for a reason. The claim that controls the Court's decision in these cases is that polygamy *really is* morally wrong. This in turn likely drives any consequentialist concerns the justices express. If polygamy is wrong, allowing it to go on somewhere in society might corrupt the innocent, and the practice might spread. This is something law should prohibit—the normalizing function of law—and therefore polygamy should not be tolerated even if it is "sanctioned by what [a] particular sect may designate as religion."

In defense of social justice

In later cases, the Supreme Court became more accommodating of religious diversity and used the free exercise clause to carve out exemptions from the requirements of otherwise valid legislation for religious groups. The pivotal case in this trend is *Sherbert v. Werner* (1963). In this case, a Seventh-Day Adventist was denied unemployment compensation because she refused to work on Saturday, her Sabbath, as required by the state's unemployment compensation act. In addressing this case, the Court tightened the defense of free exercise by holding that a state could burden this right only if it had a compelling interest in doing so and only if it used the least intrusive means available. Because the Court held that the state's interest in protecting its unemployment insurance fund failed to constitute a sufficiently compelling interest, the state's interest in the case had to yield to a fundamental liberty.

While the *Sherbert* compelling interest test set the standard for free exercise jurisprudence for some time to come, the balancing strategy employed does not necessarily indicate that this approach displays any great or commanding appreciation of the concerns of social justice. The test does not really emphasize the significance of the free exercise of religion because what the test makes significant is not religion but the significance of the state's interest juxtaposed to the free exercise of religion. As a result, the practical implication of the test, as Mark Tushnet has said, is that "the law must recognize religion only to the extent that religion has no socially significant consequences" (Tushnet, 1988, p. 264). The free exercise of religion must yield, in other words, to legislation if the issuance of an exemption would produce "socially significant consequences." While judicial intuition might have sensibly sided with free exercise in the circumstances surrounding *Sherbert*, it seems altogether probable that, had the *Davis* Court authored this test, the "socially significant consequences" of exempting the Mormon litigants from the Idaho statute would have prompted the justices to reach the same conclusion they did in fact reach.

The second case worth mentioning in the Court's heightened defense of the free exercise of religion is *Wisconsin v. Yoder* (1972). In this case the Court exempted members of the Old Order Amish from the state-mandated requirement to send their children to school through the twelfth grade. The Amish argued that pursuing formal education beyond the eighth grade was inconsistent with their religious beliefs and additional schooling beyond this point might incline Amish children to leave the faith. In finding for the Amish, the Court strengthened the *Sherbert* test by holding that the state had to demonstrate a compelling interest in not granting a religious exemption to the Amish community; no mere legitimate interest would succeed in permissibly denying the requested exemption.

The decision in *Yoder* does not overcome the problems inherent in the balancing strategy noticed above, of course, and while the case was, and remains, controversial in academic circles (Spinner, 1994, pp. 108–112; Barry, 2001, pp. 176–178), one suspects that the reasonably innocuous social presence of members of the Amish faith throughout the citizenry made a strong judicial defense of religious liberty relatively easy in this case. The Amish in the 1970s were hardly demonized in the fashion suffered by the Mormons in the latter part of the nineteenth century. If there was moral disdain for what the Amish were up to, it was confined to those liberal circles where there was concern that the Amish children were condemned by the case to an Amish life and unable to access the greater diversity available to elements of the mainstream culture (*Wisconsin v. Yoder*, 1972, pp. 245–246, Douglas J. dissenting). In short, it is hard to conclude that the case illustrates an earnest judicial effort to articulate a just resolution to a problem of religious difference because the Amish free exercise claim was generally met with public and judicial indifference. It is not terribly difficult to tolerate the Amish, by and large, because their way of life does not produce the level of moral concern in the general public that is sparked by practices like polygamy or faith healing. And the same can be said for the unemployment benefits at issue in *Sherbert*.

Civil liberties are rarely considered to be absolute, of course, and shortly we will say some things intended to elaborate on this important point. At present, we note this only to introduce the fact that things went differently for the Amish when they approached the Court with a request to be exempted from paying social security taxes on free exercise grounds (*United States v. Lee*, 1982). This case clearly raised a socially significant question, and the Court had no trouble finding in favor of the state's interest in defending its taxing power against the claim that paying taxes violated religious belief on the ground that this interest was compelling. This decision seems unassailable, even—or perhaps especially—on social justice grounds, but it is hardly evident that the compelling interest rhetoric is the best way to demonstrate the point. If social justice requires the government, including the legal system, to safeguard difference against majority disdain—as we shall argue shortly that it does—it also requires the Government to see to it that all elements of the population fulfill their obligations of citizenship, regardless of group beliefs. Being, say, Amish does not preclude one from also being an American, and a condition of being a citizen of a polity committed to respecting difference is that one meet the obligations that come with this citizenship—in this case, paying taxes.

The case of *Employment Division, Department of Human Resources of Oregon v. Smith* (1990) marked yet another judicial change of heart in the area of free exercise litigation, a change that pushes back in the direction of *Reynolds.* In *Smith*, the state of Oregon had refused to pay unemployment benefits to a Native American who had been dismissed from his job as a drug counselor because he used peyote during religious worship. Smith contended that the denial of unemployment benefits violated his right to the free exercise of religion because the state was forcing him to choose between abandoning his religious practice or suffering the lack of unemployment compensation, for which he would otherwise qualify, because of the nature of his religious practice. Following *Sherbert*, the Oregon Attorney General argued that the State had a compelling interest in overriding Smith's religious practice because peyote contains the hallucinogen mescaline that, the attorney general claimed, has substantial deleterious effects upon human physiology.

In deciding the case in favor of the State, however, the Supreme Court abandoned the *Sherbert* test and held that Smith was not constitutionally entitled to his exemption from state law because his religious practice violated a valid state law that was not designed intentionally to burden religion. In speaking for the Court, Justice Scalia emphasized that free exercise protection does not reach laws that burden religion only incidentally, and because Oregon's anti-drug legislation was not an attempt by the state to limit or obstruct the religious practices of Native Americans, it did not violate the free exercise requirement. The Court left open the possibility that a state might legislatively craft exemptions to anti-drug legislation for religious reasons if it wished to do so, and Oregon, along with several other states, eventually moved in this direction.

On its face, *Smith* looks like a substantial step backward in the judicial defense of religious difference, but in actuality, the effect of *Smith* will not likely depart substantially from outcomes that could be anticipated under the *Sherbert* test. Oregon's Attorney General had no difficulty arguing that a mescaline-infused drug could seriously harm anyone who used it, and he could support his case with substantial medical evidence. Presumably, this harm is the reason Oregon (like other states) criminalized use of such substances in the first place. Governments in the US use the mechanism of law to prevent people from harming themselves and/or others, and it is hardly far-fetched to insist that it has a substantial interest in doing so. Since this is sufficient to meet the *Sherbert* test, and since these circumstances are likely to recur in other cases involving the violation of a criminal statute, it appears that there is little practical difference between *Sherbert* and *Smith*.

This outcome may not seem altogether surprising because both lines of precedent privilege the state's function as defender of the primary norms of the dominant culture over its function as defender of social justice. In *Smith*, Oregon sought to protect Smith from harming himself, and possibly others, by using peyote. The norms of the dominant culture are in clear evidence in this case: The use of certain drugs does physiological damage to the body and may also result in significant social damage. Therefore, drugs of this sort should not be used by people, even if some individuals think it desirable to use them, perhaps because they don't understand the science of the matter or perhaps because they just don't care. Because religion, customary practice, education, family concern, and other social mechanisms for teaching and enforcing social norms within the dominant culture no longer have the reach or clout they once did, we must now rely more fully on law for their enforcement. The slow erosion of these other mechanisms of social integration places greater weight on the normalizing function of law.

Legal assertions of this sort, it is important to emphasize, are invariably put forth in general and comprehensive terms; law defends norms of the dominant culture that are presumed to hold for everyone. Their reach is comprehensive across the body politic and is not restricted to any specific cultural or religious community. Norms of this sort are not just blind to cultural difference, they also blind, or tend to blind, the population of the dominant culture to the fact of difference. The result is a blindness to the requirements of social justice that co-exist alongside norms of the dominant culture and often stand in opposition to them. It should hardly seem surprising, then, that the great American compromise involving the balancing of social justice concerns against the convictions of the dominant culture substantially favors the normalizing function of law. The toleration of difference prevails primarily when it is not juxtaposed with minority practices considered particularly odious or morally wrong by elements of the dominant culture. But it is not toleration to put up with things about which one is indifferent; toleration is present only when people put up with the intolerable (Williams, 1996, pp. 18–28).

Ironically, in *Smith* Justice Scalia was actually sensitive to the fact of religious difference in America, and this sensitivity apparently helped motivate him to turn away from the *Sherbert* test. Sticking to the notion of compelling interest, he worried, would result in "courting anarchy." "Precisely because we are a cosmopolitan nation made up of people of almost every conceivable religious preference, . . . and precisely because we value and protect religious divergence, we cannot afford the luxury of deeming presumptively invalid, as applied to the religious objector, every regulation of conduct that does not protect an interest of the highest order" (pp. 885–888). It seems Scalia was concerned for the viability of the rule of law in a divergent and pluralist population. In order to protect the rule of law, however, Scalia elected to privilege the normalizing function of law over the defense of religious toleration, and he did so at the expense of the principles of social justice which have emerged through the history of religious conflict as the best way to mediate the problem of religious pluralism.

If we resolve the great American compromise in this way, it becomes difficult to justify the authority of law to those minority groups who are required to conform to the ways of the majority culture or face the consequences. If the law's claim to authority is to be valid, law must be recognized and respected as legitimate by all members of the body politic, and this goal cannot be realized if the law is regarded as a tool of oppression by those whose ways are imposed upon by dominant religious, moral, and ideological majorities. The law's claim to authority, then, can be vindicated only if the legal system is dedicated to, and respectful of, fundamental principles of political morality capable of being accepted and endorsed by all the diverse elements of a pluralist society. This is a political morality that brings the ideal of social justice to life.

Because the great American compromise is not particularly sympathetic to the toleration of difference as a solution to the problem of pluralism, there is some reason to suppose that the prospects for realizing a cultural defense that would protect diverse cultural practices against criminal prosecution are not good. But because the great American compromise is not a particularly compelling way to address the problem of pluralism, there is reason to defend an account of social justice that might indicate a better approach to the challenges posed by the fact of normative difference. If a case can be made for a cultural defense, it should be evident that it will follow from a theory of social justice that offers support for the recognition and toleration of minority ways and practices. This is why we think it important to examine the question of a cultural defense in the more capacious theoretical manner presented in the introduction. And this is why we will return to the issue of social justice in Chapter 3 to see if we might anchor a defense of the cultural defense there.

2 The question of culture

Before turning explicitly to the prospects for a cultural defense in American criminal law, there is another preliminary matter in need of some discussion and refinement. The question of culture—its nature and place in human lives—needs to be examined. This troubling and complicated issue needs to be addressed, if only rather superficially, for two important reasons. The first is that human beings are creatures shaped mentally and/or intellectually to some presumably considerable extent by cultural factors and variables, and the second is that this shaping has direct and important implications for the way American law reaches judgments about criminal responsibility. Whether these reasons support in some way the propriety of a cultural defense remains to be seen, but the first step in exploring this matter requires us to develop a satisfactory working account of the cultural dimension of human life. That will be the focus of this chapter, and it sends us, albeit briefly, into the field of social theory.

Culture and being human

The claim that culture significantly influences and even directs human conduct may not seem terribly shocking or unbelievable to some. Yet the introduction of considerations of culture into our understanding of human beings and human action is largely foreign to the classic, and Enlightenment-inspired, conception of persons generally operative in American law. It also seems to be largely foreign to the commonplace conception of persons held by many Americans raised within a cultural context that inclines them to see persons (or at least healthy and normal adult persons) as self-determining, independent, and responsible agents. On this traditional view, human beings are rational creatures capable both of formulating and pursuing their own ends and also capable of distinguishing right from wrong and governing their behavior accordingly.

Because this familiar image tends to ennoble the individual human being as a creature of "incomparable worth," as Kant put it, it is not one that many people, including a great many scholars, wish to abandon. But in recent years it has been challenged, in more theoretical circles, by communitarian thinkers, feminist theorists, and multiculturalists, who want at least to supplement this familiar Enlightenment vision with important social facts about human attachment, sharing, and interdependence (cf. MacIntyre, 1999). But these philosophers and political theorists have only gotten onto something that has actually been a staple of modern social science for some time. It may be a bit much to say, as Gregory Starrett has, that the social sciences developed "precisely to undo the faith that our lives and selves are independent of larger social, political, economic, and cultural forces and processes" (2008, p. 272). But even if this was not a founding purpose of social science, it seems to be a lesson learned because of, and from, the efforts of social scientists. Mark Bickhard has summarized what seems to be the prevailing wisdom within contemporary social science: "The person is constituted in the multiple ways of being social that that individual has developed in that society and culture and historical time" (Bickhard, 2004, p. 126).

The insights of social science, when juxtaposed with the Enlightenment conception of the independent individual, might seem to leave us with a messy and contradictory understanding of persons. But for present purposes, the problem produced by this clash of conceptions is not that if we see persons as self-reliant individuals of the sort championed, say, by R.W. Emerson, there is little room left to recognize them as culturally situated, embedded, or contextualized beings. The problem—or fear, rather—is that if we see persons as culturally situated, embedded, or contextualized beings, then it appears that our sense of persons as responsible agents is imperiled (cf. Archer, 1995, pp. 33–65). If American jurisprudence can do rather nicely without the hyper-individualism once popular in certain social and intellectual circles, it would be hard-pressed to abandon the notion that persons are responsible agents who are properly subject to punishment for doing things that they should know they ought not do.

A culturally sensitive account of persons threatens the conception of persons as responsible agents in two ways. The first involves the familiar issue of cultural or social determinism. Descriptions of persons as "culturally embedded" or "culturally situated" beings seem to encourage the rather hasty conclusion that persons do what they do because of their culture. We might think here that persons are like computers. Human physiology, according to this analogy, resembles computer hardware, and culture resembles the software that programs a computer to do what it does. If we accept this model, then persons are determined by cultural factors to act as they do, and they could not do otherwise any more than a computer could do otherwise. But if persons are merely "cultural dopes" of this sort, as Anthony Giddens puts it, then they can hardly be responsible for their actions. They merely do what their culture would have them do.

The second threat that cultural situatedness poses for the notion of responsible agency is illustrated by postmodern concerns over the dangers of essentialism (cf. Fuss, 1990). Cultural essentialism encourages the view that persons are (largely) identical creatures who walk together in lock-step to the dictates of their culture (Archer, 1988, pp. 25–46; Lernestedt, 2014, p. 40). These cultural clones again behave according to the dictates of their culture even if these dictates display themselves in emotional outbursts that involve acting rashly from anger, fear, jealousy, or the like—and thus in ways that we might think irresponsible and inappropriate.

While cultural essentialism and cultural determinism both threaten the notion of responsible agency, they differ in important ways. Cultural essentialism is an epistemological mistake that is easily avoidable by articulating a more nuanced account of how culture influences human *being*. Cultural determinism is a theory about human being that is both controversial and difficult either to verify or falsify.[1] It is also a theory that is difficult to state clearly and cogently. As Melissa Brown has warned, efforts to appeal to culture in order to explain human behavior can easily lead to an empty tautology. "People do what they do because of culture, but culture is what people do" (Brown, 2008, p. 7). Why, then, should we think that culture *determines* individual conduct? Why not insist, instead, that individual conduct *determines* culture?[2] Zygmunt Bauman also makes a similar point when he describes culture as "self-determined determination" (Bauman, 1999, p. xiii).

However, the mistake of cultural essentialism is avoidable, and the appeal (if it has any) of cultural determinism suitably weakened, if the concept of culture is understood as "an intellectual construct used for describing (and explaining) a complex cluster of human behaviors, ideas, emotions, and artifacts" (Borofsky, 2008, p. 281). Regarded as a term of art in this way, the notion of culture is not misidentified as a thing (with an essence) that is inconsistent with another thing, namely individual agency, and that programs yet another thing, namely the human body. Instead, the notion of culture thus construed describes a certain social milieu within which agency operates.

The feature of this general milieu that we shall be most concerned with involves the raw data of belief and normative conviction that people examine, consider, critique, debate, amend, and eventually commit to or revise. These data have a physical presence in the corpus of intelligibilia (books, films, documents, etc.) as well as a mental or intellectual presence in the minds of the persons who belong to a particular cultural community. For present purposes, however, we shall not make much of this distinction. In either case, people do not necessarily possess culture naively or unreflectively (though no doubt many do); instead the social data, or at least a great deal of the data, that constitute what social scientists call culture, are the subject of human scrutiny, curiosity, reflection, conflict, and recreation, although in reflecting upon their social world—its norms, rules, beliefs, customs, practices, traditions, and so forth—people do not often overtly recognize that they are reflecting upon (aspects of) their culture (cf. Bauman, 1999, p. xiv). Consequently, the tautology that Brown has noticed need not seem all that empty because people do not necessarily act mechanically on cultural influences; nor are they necessarily unwitting products of the social world around them.

People are no doubt influenced by the cultural factors that they internalize as a consequence of growing *into* a particular kind of social system, but what they do, or how they "go on" both individually and collectively will in turn reconstruct this culture (Bauman, 1999, p. xxxv; Giddens, 1984, p. 171). The relation between persons and culture, we are suggesting, is dynamic, largely because the beliefs and norms inherited as a dimension of culture are invariably underdetermined. The underdetermined character of inherited beliefs and norms requires the re-examination and re-articulation of these social data as they are applied by persons in the process of living a life, and the result is often the revision and (typically modest) reconstruction of these data as persons come to grips with their inheritance. If this were not the case, social change would not be possible (cf. Elder-Vass, 2012, pp. 46–47). On this scenario, culture influences individual conduct, but it does not determine it. The process of *learning* the beliefs and *grasping* the norms of one's culture implies agency, as does the process of "going on" associated with internalizing and acting upon these norms.

So there is reason to think that the notion of agency is entirely consistent with—and perhaps even entails—the view that persons are culturally situated beings. And if human agency can be reconciled with a conception of persons as culturally situated beings, it is not difficult to see how the notion of responsibility for one's actions can also be reconciled with this conception of persons. Learning the beliefs and norms of one's culture involves inheriting ways of seeing and being that, by their nature, inform, govern, and direct one's conduct. There is an obvious analogy here to learning the rules of a game. In learning the game of chess, one learns that one must move the pieces in a particular way, and the violation of these rules of play has negative consequences. Similarly, in learning to live with others, one learns the rules of association that govern the interpersonal relationships characteristic of one's culture, and the violation of these rules also has negative consequences within one's cultural community. Cultural norms get reinforced by virtue of their enforcement by the community.

It is difficult to imagine a cultural community that does not reinforce its interpersonal norms of association in this way, and thus it is difficult to imagine a cultural community that does not have some sense of responsible behavior. Responsibility of this sort is a way of impressing upon independent agents that there are consequences for actions that do not follow the "rules of the game," so to speak. If this is right, then the notion of culture, understood as a term of art within the social sciences in the fashion introduced above, does not exclude, or render incoherent, the idea of responsible agency. Instead, the understanding of persons as responsible agents at home in the dominant contemporary American culture (and built into American criminal jurisprudence), is entirely consistent with, and may even entail, a conception of persons as culturally situated beings.

Conceptions of culture

In the remainder of the discussion, we shall use the notion of culture as a term of art of the sort introduced above. Some social scientists and social theorists avoid the term "culture" in favor of the familiar sociological notion of "social structure" (cf. Giddens, 1979; Giddens, 1984), but others contend that the way these two notions are used in social thought overlap substantially (cf. Sewell, 1992; D'Andrade, 2008). There is reason to preserve the notion of culture for present purposes, however, because the concept is integral to the way the subject at hand is discussed within the legal context. It should become clear as the discussion progresses that the meaning of culture adopted here is both consistent with, and appropriate for, the general debate regarding a cultural defense in criminal jurisprudence.

Accordingly, to say that persons are cultural beings is to say that they belong to at least one social milieu that provides them with an inheritance that influences the way they understand and operate within their world—the world as identified for them by their culture. Thus the word "culture" operates as a place-holder representing what Borofsky calls a "complex cluster of human behaviors, ideas, emotions, and artifacts" (Borofsky, 2008, p. 281). If we are to understand the full implications of the claim that persons are culturally situated beings, however, we need to say a bit more about this cluster. It is necessary, in particular, to have some sense of the way culture influences and shapes individual human lives.

To start, it is worth noting that the notion of culture matters politically because it is, as Marxists might put it, a concept in antagonism. Culture, like the notion of class, must be understood in opposition to something else; the notion differentiates, and thus also associates, according to specific criteria. It is not possible to have just one culture, just as it is not possible to imagine a society with only a single class. If all human social life were culturally homogeneous, there would be no work for the concept of culture to do. There would be no differentiation between human beings that could be understood or classified in terms of the notion of culture.

Class divisions, as displayed for example in the works of Aristotle or Marx, are not cultural divisions; divisions of wealth of the sort that differentiate classes are consistent with considerable cultural homogeneity. And needless to say, there are numerous other ways to differentiate between persons (e.g., race, height, intellectual or athletic ability) that do not count as cultural differentiations. But cultural differences between peoples are common enough, and we do not really need the social sciences in order to recognize them. States that comprehend substantial cultural differentiation qualify as pluralist states precisely because of this differentiation. Politically speaking, then, the problem of pluralism can be understood largely, though perhaps not entirely, as a product and feature of cultural differentiation.

This might seem to put things too strongly. Other human factors differentiate as well—consider for example race, ethnicity, nationality, religion, language, and perhaps group history, and these may also be the source of the intergroup conflict that is politically troubling and challenging within pluralist states (cf. Carr, 2006, pp. 56–61). But the relation between culture and these other factors remains obscure, and, depending upon what we mean by each of them, some or all might be comprehended by the notion of culture. This, however, is not an issue that will be explored in any great detail here. It is sufficient for present purposes to note that cultural differentiation is a significant aspect of the problem of pluralism that must be addressed by the political and legal systems of pluralist states.

It might be desirable at this point to offer a definition of culture that would help identify and clarify the nature of the differentiation (and hence association) between persons signified by recourse to the notion of culture. The general desire for definitions, however, seems to be a legacy of a familiar positivism that refuses to die even though it misleads, at least in this case, by suggesting that culture is something that exists independently of persons and needs to be defined in order to be recognized. Perhaps, however, enough has been said already to deflect this problem as a cause for concern. And while political (and legal) theory may not need a nuanced social scientific account of culture in order to recognize its political salience, something like this sort of account seems required if we are to appreciate fully the nature of the conflict that produces the problem of pluralism. It might prove profitable, then, to focus, albeit briefly, on how the notion of culture is used by thinkers intent upon identifying or accounting for differentiations of social processes, institutions, structures, and modes of social being among groups of persons that qualify as distinct when measured by these social standards.

When we look at the kinds of concerns that frequently recur in the copious literature on culture, three themes become apparent: comprehensiveness, sharing, and cultivation. First among these is the notion of comprehensiveness; culture comprehends basically all significant beliefs, norms, and ideals in a social order bounded and identified by the fact that these things matter to this group of people (D'Andrade, 2008, p. 28). Consider, for example, the comprehensive account of culture introduced by Bhikhu Parekh:

> Culture refers to a body of beliefs and practices in terms of which a group of individuals understand and organize their lives. It includes their views on the natural and the human world, their values and ideals, their expectations of each other, their notions of rationality and forms of reasoning, their manner of structuring human relations, the meaning and significance they assign to different human activities, and so on.
>
> (2014, p. 108)

If all this is comprehended by the notion of culture, then culture is pervasive and resembles what Wittgenstein referred to (no doubt with intended ambiguity) as a "form of life" (Wittgenstein, 1958, p. 226e). And if this account aptly represents our general sense of the pervasiveness of culture, it seems fair to say that culture sinks deeply into the fabric of human *being*. The fundamental ways of seeing and doing, thinking and understanding, that characterize a human life are gleaned, at least initially, from the store of social data constitutive of a person's culture and become this person's social inheritance.

But accounts of this sort invariably stumble into some tumultuous and disputatious waters. One might ask, for example, if culture really shapes a group's sense of rationality or form of reasoning. Is rationality really culturally relative, as Parekh's comments seem to suggest, or is it a standard capacity of persons that holds across all of humankind (cf. Winch, 1972, pp. 8–49; Hollis & Lukes, 1982)? And we might also wonder if this "body of beliefs and practices" exists independently of persons, as Durkheim is famously said to have claimed (Durkheim, 1964, p. 3), or if it is epiphenomenal upon human consciousness. If it exists independently of persons, where exactly is it, and how does it get internalized by the group of persons whose lives it organizes? Or if culture exists only because consciousness exists, how does it shape the consciousness that brings it into being?

Perhaps we can appeal here to something like Margaret Archer's "corpus of existing intelligibilia" from which cultural meaning is somehow learned or extracted (Archer, 1988, p. 104). Archer's intelligibilia form an archive of material things—the books, documents, and the like, mentioned previously—that provide the physical mechanisms supporting the transference of the beliefs and norms constitutive of a group's culture from one generation to the next. Recourse to an archive, however, does not explain how these beliefs and understandings are learned or fathomed by those subject to the process of enculturation; nor does it address the apparent problem posed by cultural communities that do not have such an objective archive. It is not difficult to imagine pre-literate societies that have as yet not developed anything like an official archive, but it does seem difficult to imagine a society of persons, pre-literate or otherwise, that lacks a cultural identity.

These and related issues, if pursued, would push us deep into the murky realm of social ontology. It might be necessary, of course, to brave this realm, at least to some modest degree, in order to appreciate how cultural difference generates aspects of the problem of pluralism. On this score, it is a salutary aspect of Parekh's account of culture that it sensitizes us to the fact that humans are always and invariably cultural beings, and that differences that produce political conflict often involve clashes of culture. But the comprehensiveness Parekh builds into his account of culture seems overly extreme and misleading. We are left with a picture of distinct and exceptionally homogeneous groups that differ from one another to the core.

This exaggerates on two fronts: first, it exaggerates the differences that separate cultures, and second, it exaggerates the homogeneity that is typically present within cultural communities. If cultural communities are as distinct as Parekh seems to suggest—if, for example, they possessed different views of rationality and forms of reasoning, then, but for happy coincidence, there could be no common standard of agreement that would make inter-cultural understanding or mutual coexistence possible. Such extraordinary and comprehensive difference would mean that disparate cultural communities—again, but for happy coincidence—would be incompatible to the core; they would exist as strangers to one another who could barely recognize, if in fact they could recognize, each other as fellow human beings.

On the other side of the coin, Parekh's sense of culture seems to leave little room for intracultural difference or subcultural variation. He is clear that values and ideals are integral aspects of culture and are transmitted to new generations through a process of enculturation. Presumably, some of these values help shape what people recognize as their religious convictions, and consequently if culture is comprehensive in the fashion apparently imagined by Parekh, religion would be a dimension of culture. But consider again Roger Williams's famous break with the elders of Massachusetts Bay. The break gave rise to a new Protestant sect in Providence Plantations with certain religious and political beliefs that were quite distinct from those of the Bay. But did it also give rise to a new cultural community, in spite of the fact that in most ways, other than religion and politics, Providence continued to resemble Boston to a considerable extent?

Here, as elsewhere, we should say, with Wittgenstein, that we do not find boundaries; we draw them. There is a mass of empirical evidence that suggests that cultural groups are not as opaque to one another as the doctrine of cultural comprehensiveness would seem to imply, just as there is a mass of empirical evidence that indicates cultural communities are not nearly as homogeneous in belief and conviction as the doctrine of cultural comprehensiveness would appear to suggest. What does seem to be the case, and what seems to be the point behind the claim of cultural comprehensiveness, is that the notion of culture is used to identify and isolate that package of belief and conviction that persons initially inherit from the social setting in which they are raised and into which they are socialized—which of course amounts to the same thing.

To this picture we should perhaps add the social fact that in many pluralist societies cultural intersectionality (intercultural influencing) is a constant feature of life. As a result, substantial cultural homogeneity is even less likely to be on display in cultural communities that coexist within pluralist social settings. Some of these communities may seek to sequester themselves in order to avoid the cultural contamination produced by the fact of intersectionality. But even here, cultural cross-fertilization is a strong possibility. Consequently, individual lives are often typified by association or identification with a number of distinct cultural influences. This should be understood to mean that the package of norms and beliefs that a person comes to hold are actually shaped by their association with different cultural groups.

This remark has rather obvious ontological and political implications. With the doctrine of cultural comprehensiveness strongly qualified in the fashion presented above, the notion of culture is now employed to identify norm systems that occupy a place of significance in the lives of the individuals holding these systems. This permits us to speak of different types of culture, where the differentiation identified involves disparate norm systems that play specific but different roles in individual lives. Thus such things as social tradition, ethnic custom, religion, morality, and even politics can and frequently do identify unique norm systems, each of which exhibits its own cultural dimension. This is a claim of social ontology that matters politically, for politics may involve a norm system that establishes the framework for the mutual and peaceful coexistence of norm systems that might come into conflict in the absence of a political understanding that makes this possible. This would produce a political culture capable of comprehending other cultural differences (different and possibly conflicting norm systems) and thus resolving the problem of pluralism at least to the extent that it is fueled by cultural difference.

But the political significance of this social ontology does not end here, for it also helps expose the normative and epistemological difference that produces the problem of pluralism in the first place. Normative viewpoints and/or belief systems considered trivial or insignificant rarely produce difference of the sort that becomes politically salient. Conflict arises only when persons differ over things that matter, perhaps substantially, because they are considered of great normative importance. Group differentiations based upon strangeness—cultural differences considered odd or bizarre by outsiders—need not produce conflict beyond the suspicion and angst that strangeness often elicits. But differentiations based upon conflicting and hostile religious, moral, and even ideological perspectives can, and all too frequently do, generate social conflict. This point is of some importance for the cultural defense issue because it indicates that it is normative difference, and not simply cultural difference, that matters here. While accounting for this difference in terms of cultural variation might be an effective way to conceptualize the matter, the introduction of the notion of culture, at this point, should not deflect attention from the fact that it is normative and epistemological difference that drives the problem of pluralism. It is the politics that cultures produce, rather than the sociology of culture, that really matters when considering the cultural defense.

This point leaves us with a political account of cultural differentiation that indicates how the concerns of culture will be understood (as a term of art) throughout the discussion to follow. Cultural differentiation exists when normative communities (groups of persons sharing similar norm systems) hold different and conflicting views that produce some degree of animosity, antagonism, or conflict between their members. These differences, in other words, are regarded as politically salient. Consider again the question whether Roger Williams's Providence was culturally distinct from Massachusetts Bay. Politically speaking, we want to say these are distinct cultural communities, in spite of the many similarities their members shared, because the normative differences that separated them were politically salient in the minds of both groups. Normative disagreement that is not politically salient in this way need not indicate cultural difference, though it can do so if both groups conceptualize the disagreement in terms of cultural difference.

Norm systems and sharing

The second general theme that recurs in sociological and anthropological accounts of culture is sharing. The sharing referred to here, of course, is not like the sharing on display when, say, two people share a piece of pie. The sharing at issue in accounts of culture can be identified by noticing that the beliefs, views, values, ideals, and expectations that Parekh mentions in his account of culture are shared among a certain group of individuals. This collection of individuals constitutes a group precisely because they share these things. What they share both binds them together and separates them from others, who are others by virtue of the fact that they do not share these things.

The sharing on display in these groups does not necessarily imply intimacy or familiarity among their members, nor, of course, does it exclude this. Groups that qualify as such by virtue of the fact that their members share certain beliefs, values, ideals, and expectations—norm systems in effect—may be quite large, and members may be strangers to one another in the sense that they do not necessarily know one another. They are not strangers to one another, however, in the sense that their ways, practices, ideals, and so forth—the practical manifestation of shared norm systems—are or seem strange to each other. Persons who are strangers in this latter sense are strange to one another because they do not share at least some practices, customs, traditions, or ways; that is, they do not share the attributes of a common culture. Strangeness of this sort is evident even in social environments where the members of different groups know and interact with one another, for familiarity does not eliminate strangeness, though it may render this strangeness commonplace and perhaps more benign because of this.

Unfortunately, these generalities do not do much to heighten an understanding of culture, and for reasons that may be apparent, given our discussion of comprehensiveness. Appeal to a sense of sharing, like the similar appeal to comprehensiveness, may produce an exaggerated and misleading sense of cultural homogeneity (Borofsky, 2008, p. 282). Roger Williams and his friends at Providence Plantations shared a great deal in common with the Puritan community in Boston, but this otherwise exceptional sharing was hardly sufficient to overcome the normative difference that separated them. The fact of sharing, in other words, may be less important to a coherent sense of culture than concerns about the relative importance of some of the beliefs and norms that are shared. Presumably, for example, commitment to the miracle of transubstantiation matters more to Catholics, and does more to fix what it means to be Catholic, than does belief in the doctrine of Papal infallibility.

According to the standard of political salience introduced above, groups are considered distinct when their members agree about the nature or importance of certain norms or beliefs sufficiently to think they are kindred spirits. But these groups may also be composed of individuals who share very little except a commitment to the nature or importance of certain norms or beliefs. Catholics can disagree with one another on many issues, and some of these will no doubt drive intra-group politics. But there are some things about which they cannot disagree and still remain Catholic. This indicates that groups we may want to consider cultural communities need not share much in common, but they cannot tolerate any and all manner of difference and disagreement. Groups split apart, in what might be called a process of group mitosis, when their internal politics lead some members to conclude that they no longer share key components of the norm system of the group. In this sense, the question of when some generally shared norm system constitutes a cultural community, or when the sharing is just an overlap between similar cultural communities, is really a political and not an ontological one.

The issue of sharing raises problems for an understanding of culture that flow in the opposite direction as well. The sharing of certain norms that matter to those who share these things cannot be restricted to cultural communities alone. Sharing of this sort is also on display in any manner of associations, collectivities, and organizations that hardly qualify as cultural groups. Athletic teams, orchestras, fraternities and sororities, bridge clubs, classic car clubs, and the like, all share certain norm systems that produce bonds of identification amongst their members, but they fall rather short of being cultures. Perhaps the apparent difficulties here can be avoided if we insist that associations and organizations of this sort are actually aspects or instances of the practices and activities characteristic of certain cultures. Athletic teams exist, for example, in cultures that value athletic competition, sportsmanship, physical activity, and so forth, while classic car clubs are possible only in cultures that have for some time relied upon cars for transportation and accepted them as symbols and icons of valued cultural ways of living.

But this response merely returns us to our previous problem, for while it is true that many people value athletic competition or enjoy classic cars, in those places where these things exist, it is also most likely true that not all the people who live in these places will value or enjoy these things or share in the enthusiasm that some people have for them. Do these people belong to different cultures? Or does culture present those who belong to it with disparate norm systems that these people can select from in the process of putting a life together? Both questions could be answered in the affirmative, of course, but if the second question is answered affirmatively, it becomes unclear why sharing should matter greatly to an account of culture. Additionally, even if we grant that athletics is a common activity within something called American (popular) culture, it would seem odd to insist that an otherwise typical American, regardless of personal history, who does not enjoy, follow, or participate in athletic activity of some sort does not for this reason actually belong to this culture.

While it seems sensible to suppose that culture involves shared norm systems, it is less evident that we can formulate a profitable account of culture by relying too heavily upon this notion alone. But some of the difficulties encountered might be averted if we supplement the discussion with an examination of the third commonly mentioned aspect of culture, namely, the notion of cultivation. If "culture" is a term that designates groups of persons identifiable (to themselves and others) by virtue of certain distinctive norm systems that they hold/share, then (as the notion implies) culture presumably involves the *cultivation* within some collection of persons of these norm systems. This is hardly a new or remarkable idea, of course; societies, as we know, perpetuate themselves. And they can do this only if one generation transfers, deliberately or otherwise, to the next the norm systems that are operative there (cf. Bourdieu, 1990; Giddens, 1984).

What gets transferred from one generation to the next, or cultivated by one generation in the next, is *culture*—or the norm systems operative in some group of persons united (loosely or generally) by them. The classic problem of social theory is to explain how this transference is made, or how culture is cultivated. Archer's "corpus of existing intelligibilia" (1988, p. 104) may be a necessary element of this transference, but it would seem to require a good deal of human support to get the job done. This, in any event, is the view of Dave Elder-Vass who attempts to explain enculturation in terms of what he calls "norm circles" (2010; 2012). Elder-Vass defines a norm circle as "a group of people who are committed to endorsing and enforcing a particular norm" (2012, p. 22; see also 2010, p. 127). The notion of sharing is again integral to Elder-Vass's notion of culture. "Unless our practices are shared they are not culture, and they can only be shared if we are all somehow influenced to follow common practices" (2012, p. 39). The influence is supplied, he argues, by norm circles. "Culture is not simply belief, but socially endorsed belief, and that social endorsement can only be brought about by the group—a norm circle" (2012, p. 44).

The introduction of norm circles to account for social enculturation may not seem terribly remarkable to most readers, for sociologists and anthropologists have supposed for some time that something like them must be operative if the intergenerational transference of social norms is to be possible. But Elder-Vass advances the notion in order to address a familiar problem of social ontology: How can we explain the fact that social norms and beliefs shape individual consciousness without also reifying them? The notion of a norm circle enables Elder-Vass to respond to this question by holding that persons shape the consciousness of others by initiating them into ways of living structured in terms of a set of beliefs and norms. Social norms exist for Elder-Vass in the minds of individuals and thus have no independent existence of their own (2012, p. 255). They are transferred from what we might think of as advocates to neophytes through the process of endorsement and enforcement that Elder-Vass contends is used by the group of advocates (norm circle) for this purpose.

In order for a norm circle to exist, some collection of individuals must share some norm in the sense that each is committed to the norm—committed, at least officially, to endorsing the norm to others and sanctioning those who fail to adhere to or subscribe to it. Neophytes who happen to be within the sphere of influence of some norm circle are thus likely to internalize the norm and become perpetuating players in the process by which the norm is reinforced and promulgated into the future. Sharing the norm in question is just the result of coming to hold the norm by virtue of one's initiation into the norm circle that is committed collectively to the norm.

Culture and action-guiding norms

The largely political account of culture introduced above can now be supplemented by stipulating that groups that share politically salient norm systems also naturally qualify as norm circles in the sense employed by Elder-Vass because they will almost certainly endorse and enforce the norms considered salient. This is necessary for two basic reasons: first, the norm circle emphasizes the practical side of culture, and second, the notion of a norm circle is compatible with both centralized and decentralized social systems. These two aspects of norm circles are important for understanding the significance cultural norms have for the lives of those who subscribe to them and for appreciating the challenges individuals often face in applying or following the norms they have learned in the process of living with others.

The practical dimension of norm circles is illustrated by the fact that norms guide and control conduct; they structure the standards of social interaction and produce the possibility of social activity. Many norms are connected intimately with beliefs, for beliefs typically underlie and power the reasons used for their support and defense. But many are also connected intimately with social practices because a social practice can be understood, in fairly traditional fashion, as an "organized constellation of actions" that is normatively governed (Schatzki, 2002, p. 71). To have a culture, then, is to possess (and share) as an inheritance a set of politically salient action-guiding norms that informs its possessor how to act (what to do and how to be with others) in certain spheres of social life that are understood to be of importance to the possessor of these norms (Elster, 1989, p. 249). Cultures (norm circles sharing salient norms) indicate to persons what matters and what sort of normative weight gets assigned to certain kinds of activities, actions, and action plans operative within their domain. Cultures, in short, orient persons normatively in the social (and physical) world and provide them with a sense of identity by connecting them to certain others and separating them from still others.

These remarks might seem to drift back toward social determinism and/or cultural essentialism, but another virtue of the notion of a norm circle is that it enables us to appreciate the point behind generalities of this sort without the need to accept either of these positions. According to Elder-Vass's account of a norm circle, each norm a person holds has a norm circle behind it that endorses and enforces the norm within the community. In principle, every norm a person holds may be supported by its own independent norm circle, but in practice it seems reasonable to think that some circles actually endorse and enforce clusters of norms. This does not imply that these clusters are comprehensive in the sense that they include all the norms a person will hold, however, or that there is no normative difference within the norm circle that endorses and enforces a particular cluster of norms. A norm circle may be united in its commitment to some cluster of norms and yet be divided with regard to a variety of other norms.

Elder-Vass takes the notion of a norm circle from Georg Simmel "because he uses it to denote over-lapping or *cross-cutting* social groups" (2010, p. 122, emphasis in original). This represents rather nicely the fluid boundaries of norm circles along with the manner in which persons will likely belong to various social groups (or cultural communities) characterized by the cluster of norms that their members endorse and enforce. He also elaborates on his notion of a norm circle by distinguishing between proximal norm circles—the "set of actual individuals who have influenced" a person to embrace some norm (2010, p. 127), and actual norm circles—the "interlinked individuals who would in fact tend to endorse and enforce the norm concerned" for and against others (2010, p. 128).

Beyond the norm in question, there is no necessary structure to the relationship between proximal and actual norm circles. A proximal norm circle, for example, may not endorse and enforce any norm cluster, and if not, it would be a collection of persons who happen to endorse and enforce a particular norm for and against some specific collection of persons. But there may be a subset of such a norm circle that does endorse and enforce a cluster of norms for and against some person. Norm circles of this sort will likely be composed of a person's parents, relatives, and friends, along with the recognized group authorities within those social institutions to which a person belongs (e.g., teachers, ministers, coaches, etc.). But the norm cluster endorsed and enforced by this circle need not have an actual norm circle that also endorses and enforces this particular cluster of norms; instead, the various norms belonging to this particular cluster may belong to a variety of actual norm circles.

The overlapping and cross-cutting that characterizes the relationships between norm circles means that persons may, and most likely will, belong to numerous actual norm circles. This is but another way to express the problems associated with thinking of cultural communities (norm circles) as comprehensive, for comprehensiveness implies that a vast majority (at least) of the norms a person holds is endorsed and enforced by a single actual norm circle. While this might hold true in unusually homogeneous and perhaps rather isolated communities, it would seem to be an extremely rare social condition. In pluralist settings, however, disparate social influences encourage intersectionality and generally guarantee that persons will belong to a variety of norm circles, though not all these need involve the endorsing and enforcing of politically salient norms. Those norm circles that do not endorse and enforce politically salient norms simply fail to qualify as cultural communities and may be viewed instead as associations and the like.

It is also possible, and rather instructive, to envision civil association in terms of an absolute norm circle that encompasses all the other actual norm circles present in the body politic. Even pluralist states will qualify as loose cultural communities if the citizenry shares a norm cluster, composed of basic political ideals that are collectively endorsed and enforced amongst them.[3] These states may be considered *loose* cultural communities because the action-guiding norms constitutive of the political norm cluster will necessarily leave substantial room for the operation and coexistence of other norm systems (cultural communities) that might be present in the state. If states exhibit a high degree of social difference of the sort that produces the problem of pluralism, they will need to be fairly loose cultural communities because they will need to comprehend a sizeable number of other cultural communities that also claim a place of prominence in the hearts and minds of the citizenry. In the modern world, states that attempt to be comprehensive cultural communities are likely to seem totalitarian and tyrannical both to outsiders and to internal dissidents.

This brings us to the second reason why it is necessary to supplement our account of culture by regarding cultural communities as norm circles, for thinking of these groups as norm circles raises important questions about their political structure. Norm circles that are committed to endorsing and enforcing norm clusters or systems may be either centralized or decentralized, depending upon their reliance on a central authority charged with policing the endorsement and enforcement of the norms constituting the cluster. Some norm circles are, or at least seem to be, completely decentralized. The standards of etiquette that are generally operative throughout the US lack any centralizing and governing authority, while law is more centralized by virtue of the secondary rules of adjudication and change, noticed by Hart, that transform customary practice into a system of law. But even the presence of official, centralized authorities to endorse and enforce some norm cluster supported by a norm circle does not preclude some degree of decentralized support for the norm system in question. Legal authorities are charged with enforcing the law, but it helps if those subject to the law respect the rule of law and encourage others to be law-abiding citizens.

Centralization is often driven by size; the larger an actual norm circle, the greater the need for a central authority in order to sustain a common commitment to the norm system it endorses and enforces—to motivate proximal norm circles in effect. But it can also be driven by the need for standardization produced by the underdetermined nature of the meaning of norms. To some extent, the need for centralization is conditional upon the nature of the norms at issue. All norms control actions and activities, but they do not all do so in the same way. The rules (norms) that control the playing of a game such as chess, for example, differ from rules (norms) that regulate proper standards of interpersonal conduct (cf. Searle, 1969, pp. 22–42). If one wants to play chess, one must follow the rules, but the norms that regulate interpersonal conduct are generally not conditional in this way. They hold against persons unconditionally or categorically, and consequently, it is of some importance in those communities or societies where such rules are in force that people learn how to apply and follow them. Here standardization matters, but the adherence to such norms is never an entirely mechanical process.

If life is lived in large measure by following norms, engaging in social practices, and the like (and not just acting upon interests and desires), doing so is not always straightforward or uncontroversial. Centralization can help take some of the guesswork out of deciding when to follow a particular norm, and it can help—but help only—remove some of the problems produced by disparate constructions or understandings of specific norms. Centralization helps in this regard by providing an authoritative account of the norm at issue, and thus providing members of the actual norm circle some inkling of when and how to follow the norm. In this fashion, centralization helps—but helps only—reduce some of the friction and uncertainty produced by the underdetermined nature of certain norms.

This underdetermination means that the precise requirements of a norm are likely uncertain and controversial. Because of underdetermination, the implications of a norm are not always clear to those who do the endorsing and enforcing of these norms within a particular norm circle. This produces possible controversy and the potential for conflict into even the most intimate norm circles, and this is the sort of thing that helps drive intragroup mitosis and social change. Proximal norm circles may with time develop their own interpretations of some politically salient norm, and this may drive conflict and possible change within the actual norm circle. The issues that separated Roger Williams and John Cotton, for example, may be critiqued in this way.

The trend toward centralization is thus a natural feature of the need for cultural communities (absolute norm circles) to resolve disputes and clarify meanings regarding the norms they share. But pressure to centralize may also promote the possibility of group mitosis if factions within the norm circle take exception to the construction or interpretation of the norms endorsed and enforced by norm circle elites. This returns us to the theme of politics and to the fluid nature of norm circles, for cultural communities, as should be apparent, will likely have their own internal political issues and conflicts. Group mitosis is likely to occur if conflicting norm construction becomes politically salient in a way that splits the norm circle and drives apart the competing parties.

Social change and political stability, these remarks intimate, are the warp and woof of social life. The problem of pluralism is seemingly an inevitable by-product of the work of norm circles, and this is perhaps the strongest point that can be pressed to expose the mistakes associated with claims of cultural essentialism and cultural or social determinism.

Culture and morality

Culture matters to human beings because it is constituted by norms that matter importantly to them. Some of these norms help inform and direct individual action, and others govern and structure interpersonal relationships. Culture comprehends the cluster or system of norms that make social life possible, and the fact that human beings make and replicate their own cultures goes some distance toward explaining why social life does not decay into a state of nature. But culture is also a messy business, largely because of the decentralized nature of social life and the underdetermination of the norms endorsed and enforced within cultural communities. Consequently, there is a good deal to be said for Steven Lukes's observation that "the idea that values come in stable, integrated, mutually exclusive configurations called 'cultures' is seriously mistaken in accounting for how the world works" (Lukes, 2008, p. 112). But if this introduces yet another reason to avoid the dangers associated with cultural essentialism, it does not indicate that we should abandon the notion of culture altogether. It is still possible to use the notion in order to identify norm clusters, perhaps roughly understood, that matter to some collection of persons (norm circle) in the sense that they provide these persons with standards of association and interaction and drive the practices in which they engage with one another.

Individual actions are largely, perhaps even massively, shaped and influenced by those action-guiding norms endorsed and enforced by those norm circles that introduce meaning and purpose into individual lives. But while it is difficult to underestimate the importance of cultural embeddedness for understanding what persons do, there is still little reason to suppose that persons are merely cultural dopes who behave in the fashion determined for them by cultural norms and practices. An explanation for this has already been discussed; it follows as a logical feature of the underdetermination of action-guiding norms. But this explanation can be supplemented by exploring further the notion of a norm circle as the endorser and *enforcer* of the norm or norm cluster that help identify a particular cultural community.

The process of producing adherence to, and general acceptance of, social norms does not resemble the job of programming a computer. Persons are able to question norms and wonder why it is important to follow or accept them. Sometimes the reasons offered by norm circle endorsers simply indicate that this is how things are done. (If you want to play chess, you must move the knight thus and so.) But at other times reasons constrain in the sense that they direct action by blocking or disallowing other actions that a person might be inclined to undertake. Regulatory norms that work in this manner indicate both what one should do and what one should *not* do, but they still require reasons that indicate why one should accept, endorse, and follow them. Sometimes these reasons are embedded within social convention, but at other times they are produced by social institutions that exercise authority through the strategy of centralization.

In both cases, of course, it is important for norm circles to be able to account for the authoritative status of the reasons advanced as endorsers and enforcers of norms. We have already discussed the way the law's claim to authority can be vindicated; at the moment we want to notice one way in which authoritativeness is conferred upon more decentralized norm systems. This involves recognizing the special character or status certain norm systems are understood to have, a status that indicates their social important to those subject to them. The norms commonly associated with standards of etiquette by the dominant cultural community in the US, for example, may be grouped under a normative concern for politeness. Social integration is thus facilitated by learning first that being polite matters in one's dealings with others and then learning how to be polite—or what norms control or regulate the process of being polite. But norms of etiquette don't carry the same normative weight that moral norms do, and this indicates that cultural communities may rank their norm systems according to norms indicating greater or lesser social importance and normative significance.

These degrees of normative importance speak to the social force behind the process of norm endorsement and enforcement, and return us to the notion of political salience that characterizes our account of cultural communities. Standards of etiquette are illustrative of good manners, but they are also generally acknowledged to be lodged in social convention only. Because of this, their normative significance, while important, falls rather short of the requirements of morality. To indicate that a particular norm is a *moral* norm, for example, is to accord it the most powerful source of social endorsement and enforcement available; these norms are highly politically salient. Good manners indicate politeness and perhaps good upbringing, but moral norms obligate. To say this is to indicate that they hold against persons in the most powerful of ways, and they may do so for some cultural communities because they are advertised as, and thus understood to be, universally and objectively true and incontrovertible.

As we have seen, however, cultural communities are distinguishable from one another because they share differing, and possibly competing and/or conflicting (incompatible) politically salient norm clusters. It would seem to follow, then, that they are also distinguishable (in part) because they hold differing and most likely incompatible moral viewpoints or moralities, for the notion of morality here signifies only the special salience certain norms enjoy within some actual norm circle. If this is right, then the intergroup conflict produced by these normative rivalries is based upon, and driven by, moral disagreement and the moral disdain this disagreement often produces. From a purely functional point of view, the insistence that moral norms are universally and objectively valid serves as a compelling social strategy for endorsing and enforcing certain norms that happen to matter greatly to the cultural communities (partly) defined by them.

From a specifically political perspective, the objective and universal feature of moral norms operative within certain actual norm circles does much to drive the problem of pluralism. The resultant sense of obligation to endorse and enforce such significant norms is often understood to comprehend all persons, and not just those already recognized as neophytes within one's own proximal cultural community. Thus, for example, Christian missionaries felt a considerable obligation to bring their God to the "heathens" of the new world. But where this sort of political salience drives competing cultural communities, normative rivalry and social conflict are almost sure to follow. This, too, exacerbates the problem of pluralism.

But where a commitment to the objective and universal feature of moral norms is in place, a purely functionalist account of moral norms, such as the one sketched above, is likely to be objectionable. The objection is that this view leads directly to cultural relativism, or to the view that moral truth is relative to, or conditional upon, one's culture. The objection misses its mark for reasons of logic, however, because the objective or universal truth of some norm cannot be undermined by noticing that certain cultural communities consider or regard it to be objective or universal. As Steven Lukes has pointed out, "[t]here are two ways of thinking about morality and moral norms" (Lukes, 2008, p. 19). First, one can adopt an external and descriptive view and see moral norms as cultural or social artifacts that are held and endorsed by some group of persons, and this is what we have done here. As should be apparent, these ethical codes tend to vary from group to group.

But one can also consider moral norms from inside some group of persons, so to speak, and notice that from this perspective moral norms are believed by those who endorse them to hold objectively and universally—that is, their truth is based upon reason and is not relative to the perspective of the group that holds them. Moral norms are understood from this internal perspective to hold similarly and uniformly for all persons at all times and in all places. Cultural communities typically regard their own moral (politically salient) norms in this way. This is an important aspect, again for some cultural communities, of the method through which norms are endorsed and enforced. The claim that, say, a norm against murder is objective and universal is a powerful way of endorsing it to group neophytes.

The first or descriptive view of moral norms introduced by Lukes may seem to encourage the acceptance of moral relativism (Ladd, 1973, pp. 107–129). If anthropological research discovers that there is little or no general agreement on normative matters across a number of different cultural communities, why should anyone still presume that moral norms exist that have escaped the notice of at least some of these people for all these years? With this question in place, it is easy to suppose that the insider, or normative, view of ethics merely displays an anthropological feature of ethical systems; believing in their validity, once again, functions to promote and assure their endorsement and enforcement. But these remarks do not defeat the logical claim that the truth (or validity) of a moral norm is independent of the consequences (intended or otherwise) that the belief in its truth (or validity) has for the way it is endorsed and enforced within the community.

Happily, there is no need to resolve the question of moral or cultural relativism here, for it is actually irrelevant to the problem of pluralism. The social fact of normative difference, (pluralism) coupled with the corresponding fact that this difference is often a source of significant political conflict and unrest, is all that is necessary in order to appreciate this problem. Because political conflict and unrest will continue in pluralist settings whether moral or cultural relativism is true or not, the pursuit of a remedy for the problem of pluralism is not conditioned upon answering this issue. People will go on judging cultural outsiders from the perspective afforded them by their own moral perspective, and when they do, it will continue to seem apparent to them that it is not possible to think "that all cultures are of equal moral value" (Phillips, 2007, p. 73).

While there is little reason to object to this, the political problem produced by the fact of significant normative difference throughout the body politic remains. Consequently, the need to determine what kind of policy a just state should adopt to address the resultant conflict also remains. The deep belief that one's moral norms are true, and that all persons, regardless of cultural background, should therefore respect them, does not make finding a solution to the problem of pluralism any easier, of course. But this will also continue to be the case whether moral or cultural relativism is true or not.

Notes

1 For what might be taken as a fairly attractive version of such a theory, see Dawkins (1976); see also Dennett (1995; 2003).

2 This dilemma has been the subject of considerable attention in recent years in the field of social theory (Archer, 1988, pp. 25–71).

3 It is possible also to regard political units as tight cultural communities of course, as the notion of the nation-state aptly illustrates. Indeed, the notion of culture might be traced, politically, to the Romantic movement in nineteenth-century Germany, which encouraged a more comprehensive sense of identification with one's patria, an identification conceptualized in terms of culture. Cf. Canovan 1998: 52–54.

3 Social justice and legal practice

With the background materials of the previous two chapters in place, it is time to take up the question of a cultural defense in American criminal law. As we indicated in Chapter 1, a comprehensive approach to this question is complicated by the fact that two distinct traditions in American legal practice seem to come into conflict when the prospects for a cultural defense are introduced. While the justice function of law would seem on its face to support such a defense, the normalcy function does not. On a more basic level, these traditions also complicate efforts to resolve the problem of pluralism. While the justice function would seem to allow us to address this problem by invoking standards of toleration of, and accommodation of, normative difference, the normalcy function would seem to necessitate a strategy that emphasizes the elimination (or at least minimization) of normative difference through strategies of integration and homogenization.

The apparent tension in evidence here is best resolved by attempting to identify, articulate, and defend certain first principles of civil association that have a strong claim on everyone's allegiance by virtue of the arguments that support them. This conclusion is rather commonplace within the tradition of political theory, of course, and consequently much of the argument of this chapter will be familiar to thinkers working within this field. But it introduces the purpose of this chapter, namely, the development and defense of basic principles of civil association—norms of social justice, in effect—capable of resolving the problem of pluralism and reconciling the apparent tension between the justice and normalcy functions of law.

By way of a modest disclaimer, it is worth emphasizing that turning to theoretical analysis in order to sharpen our understanding of the central norm system of American political culture cannot yield an exact, official, and uncontroversial picture of the norms linked within this system; there is no sense of "getting it right" here because a fully determined view of these norms is not floating about somewhere. Political thought can produce only theoretical constructs that are bound to be controversial and disputatious in their own right. The case for them depends upon the logical sufficiency of their derivation, and the appreciation of this point matters because a concern for the logical sufficiency of argument transforms the discourse involved from mere ideological bickering into a presumptively more profitable theoretical inquiry.

Social justice: the freedom factor

Social justice is concerned with the norms that control the basic structure of society and dictate how social goods are to be distributed throughout the population. As a result, it enjoys a reputation, aptly expressed by John Rawls, as "the first virtue of social institutions," and therefore, "laws and institutions no matter how efficient or well-arranged must be reformed or abolished if they are unjust" (Rawls, 1971, p. 3). A shared sense of social justice anchors the state to a set of ideals that transforms an otherwise eclectic and disparate collection of groups (cultural communities/norm circles) into a common polity united by "bonds of civic friendship" (Rawls, 1971, p. 5). This becomes the foundation of the political culture of the civic community identifiable in terms of the state.

Discussions of the nature and significance of social justice within the American academy (and elsewhere) have been both inspired and influenced for well over 50 years by Rawls's monumental contributions to political thought and by his justly famous notion of justice as fairness.[1] For the most part, the theoretical industry Rawls inspired has focused on two central aspects of his theory of justice: (1) the two substantive principles that he associated with social justice, and (2) the formal argument for the derivation and defense of these two principles. Rawls's first principle of justice, as originally formulated, defended "an equal right to the most extensive basic liberty compatible with a similar liberty for others" (1971, p. 60). His second principle controlled the arrangement of social and economic inequalities, and covered the distribution of income and wealth, and offices and opportunities (1971, p. 61). These two principles were presented by Rawls in lexical order to establish the priority of liberty over the more material concerns of the second principle (1971, p. 244).

Theoretical support for these two principles took the form of a thought experiment that employed a device Rawls called the "original position." He asked readers to imagine a situation (the original position) in which they must choose principles to govern the basic structure of the society in which they will eventually live, and he added that they are to make their selection from behind a veil of ignorance that shrouds from view all particular facts about themselves and their personal identity, including the particular details about the time and place in which they will live. The choosing subjects behind the veil of ignorance are, in effect, proxy persons who must imagine that they can be anyone who will live in the society to be governed by the principles they select. But these subjects do know "general facts about human society" (1971, p. 137). In fact, they "are presumed to know whatever general facts affect the choice of the principles of justice," including details about public affairs, economic theory, social organization, and human psychology (1971, p. 137).

The idea behind the original position, as Rawls explains, "is to set up a fair procedure so that any principles agreed to will be just" (1971, p. 136). The veil of ignorance guarantees that choices will not be prejudiced by privileged insight into personal talents and abilities, social position, or the like, and this assures that the selection process will be fair. The principles selected by the rational, self-interested, and (it turns out) rather risk-averse, calculators will be recognized to promote the best interests of everyone to live in the imagined society, and this assures that these rational self-interested choosers must admit that their imagined society is just.

Rawls would later retreat somewhat from the moral confidence of *Theory* and express an appreciation for what we have called the problem of pluralism. His revised strategy involved conceptualizing his theory of justice as a purely political doctrine that was not locked within or dependent upon any "comprehensive philosophical doctrine" (1993, pp. xvi–xviii). This substantial revision, influenced no doubt by the so-called multicultural movement of the 1980s and 90s, seems motivated by an emergent appreciation for the presence within society of groups of persons holding "incompatible religious, philosophical, and moral doctrines"—that is, for the fact of what he called "reasonable pluralism" (1993, p. xxiv).

The maelstrom of debate and discourse that swirled around Rawls's argument even before, but especially after, publication of *Theory* focused almost exclusively on his second principle of justice (or the problem of distributive justice) and the procedural elements of the argument involving the original position and the veil of ignorance (cf. Barry, 1973; Wolff, 1977). Substantially less attention was given to his first principle, and of those who did take this issue up (cf. Hart 1973), we have been unable to locate anyone inclined to disparage the claim that freedom is a fundamental pillar of a just state. Nor should anyone find this surprising, for as we argued in the first chapter, freedom—or at least the freedom of conscience—is a fundamental element of the liberal political morality that has emerged in the wake of the fragmentation of Christianity. A theory of justice that failed to give adequate expression to this familiar and generally cherished political norm could not presume to resonate positively with the audience to whom it was addressed.

Rawls was already aware of this point even at the time he wrote *Theory*, but he makes it explicitly in his later work. Noticing, as we did above, that religious disagreement all too frequently produced conflict over issues of the first importance to people—matters about which they could not compromise—he emphasized that such a situation "forces either mortal conflict moderated only by circumstance and exhaustion, or equal liberty of conscience and freedom of thought" (1993, p. xxvi; 303). In the absence of a commitment to these "firmly founded and publicly recognized [norms], no reasonable political conception of justice is possible" (1993, p. xxvi). Freedom of conscience was not the only element of the freedom safeguarded by his first principle, of course; he included in the mix political freedom (the suffrage plus the right to hold public office), freedom of speech and assembly, the right to own property, and "freedom from arbitrary arrest" (1971, p. 61). But he emphasized that "the question of equal liberty of conscience is settled. It is one of the fixed points of our considered judgments of justice" (1971, p. 206).

Roger Williams differs from John Rawls on this score. Rawls's political liberalism, and hence his defense of freedom of conscience, is freestanding in the sense that it is not derived from, or dependent upon, some prior comprehensive philosophical or moral theory/doctrine. This separates Williams from Rawls and a good many contemporary liberals more generally, for the latter defend a set of political norms (a political culture, in effect) that is independent of, and as Rawls would put it, prior to the various religious, moral, and ideological norm systems that have a presence in the liberal state—"prior to" in the sense that the political norms have precedence over, or trump, these other norm systems in the event of a conflict between them. Not all self-proclaimed liberals consider liberalism a political doctrine, of course; many consider it a comprehensive philosophical and moral doctrine in its own right (cf. Galston, 1991; 2005). But there is little reason to engage this much discussed issue here, other than to notice that if liberalism is taken to be a comprehensive doctrine, it is uncertain whether it can realize its enduring promise of resolving the problem of pluralism (cf. Carr, 2010, pp. 77–97). To do this, we need a doctrine flexible enough to promote norms that all the cultural communities present in the state can endorse, accept, and enforce. The only way to guarantee such flexibility (without substantial additional theoretical wrangling) is to consider liberalism a political doctrine in the fashion defended by Rawls.

The pertinence of this discussion of Rawls resides with his attractive defense of freedom of conscience, which we have suggested appears to be the central pillar supporting a just state. We propose now to attempt to update Rawls's defense of freedom of conscience and thought in order to explicate its implications for addressing the problem of pluralism. In doing so, we are not attempting to update his general theory of justice, for there is clearly more to this theory than the concern for freedom of conscience and thought. But it is the freedom of conscience that matters here, for it should be apparent from our construction of the problem of pluralism that this freedom speaks directly to it. This claim repeats the view that the political strategy that eventually brought religious freedom to prominence in the wake of the social conflict produced by the fragmentation of Christianity can serve as viable precedent for considering how best to address contemporary problems produced by the fact of cultural difference.

The update to Rawls we are imagining involves considering whether the notion of freedom of conscience that he took to be central to our general sense of social justice can be expanded or developed to embrace cultural as well as religious difference. Happily, considering this issue does not require the adoption or continuation of Rawls's theoretical strategy of argument. There is no real need to worry about an original position or a veil of ignorance, for example, because a familiarity with the "general facts" relevant to the choice of principles of justice that Rawls allowed within his initial choice situation will not only indicate what principles should be chosen but also help elaborate their reach and identify their meaning. The discussion of the previous chapter should help expose the intellectual and theoretical sources of a set of relevant facts not explicitly mentioned by Rawls. In particular, the information gleaned from social theory and cultural anthropology helps us understand the deeply social dimension of being human and appreciate the place and significance that the norm systems, captured and grouped under the notion of culture, have in shaping individual lives and socializing persons into their inherited communities.

These data, along with some general familiarity with the history of political struggle, should suffice to enable the sensible choice of principles of justice capable of addressing and managing the problem of pluralism—the specific focus of our concerns here. With this general information in place, there is no need to hypothetically shroud from view specific details about the personal lives of those faced with choosing principles of justice for the organization and management of social life. This information tells us: (1) why principles of justice (the norm system of a political culture) are necessary in the first place in order to secure social order and stability (i.e., to address the intergroup conflict produced by the fact of normative difference), and (2) why this conflict is an unavoidable and enduring aspect of the human condition. Given these sociological, anthropological, and historical desiderata, the need for the adoption of principles of *civil* association should be clear, and the theoretical restrictions on the choice of these principles should also be apparent.

The right to cultural autonomy

There are two primary sources of normative difference: the group mitosis mentioned in the previous chapter and immigration. Immigration introduces new norm circles into a host state that produce new and different ethnic, religious, linguistic, and/or ideological communities. Depending upon the extent of the differences involved—differences ranging from food, dress, and the norms that control etiquette, to the much deeper concerns of religion, morality, and cosmology—immigration brings strangeness into the land, and strangeness is a potential source of conflict. Group mitosis also produces divisive differences, as the story of Roger Williams illustrates. Groups may well fragment when preferred constructions or accounts of politically salient norms generate intractable internal conflict. Consequently, cultural communities may well break into a collection of hostile groups driven to conflict by disagreement over the meaning and significance of the norms they once shared.

To these basic sources of conflict we might add the natural evolution of groups. Established norm circles may wither and die; new norm circles may emerge, flourish for a time, and then fade into obscurity. Existing norm circles that were once indifferent to the differences separating them may become normative rivals if the evolution of their norm or norm clusters produces disagreement that becomes a source of intergroup hostility. The Ku Klux Klan in the US, for example, receives substantially less support from the remainder of the white, Protestant population of the country than it once did. Of course, this aspect of social change also works in the opposite direction—the Irish, for example, are now much less despised by non-Irish than they once were, and Catholics are less demonized by non-Catholics than they once were. When it comes to social life, it seems that uncertainty is the only real constant.

This fact of social flux will likely be sobering for anyone asked to select principles of justice in order to address the problem of pluralism. We can suppose that the choosing subjects will have a natural preference for the specific norms that matter to them—norms that they endorse and enforce, and we can suppose further that, prior to the choice of principles, toleration is unlikely to be one of the norms they endorse and enforce. Let us say that our subjects know the demographics of the society to be governed by the selection of principles of justice and that it resembles the demographics of the United States—a grouping of immigrant communities constituting minority or satellite cultures orbiting around a dominant group separated into numerous disparate norm circles of its own by virtue of the historical operation of the phenomenon of group mitosis (cf. Fuchs, 1990; Walzer, 1996; Spinner-Halev, 2000). Within this curious and complex mix, a choosing subject can hardly be confident that she or he will belong to a norm circle sufficiently dominant to be able to realize her or his interests into the future. The grim fact of social uncertainty, backed by even a modest grasp of social history, recommends against great confidence in this sort of dominance lasting through time.

This explains why someone would be willing to select principles of justice in the first place. A strategy of peaceful coexistence should be clearly preferable to the "take what comes" alternative of a "war of all against all." So the initial choice problem is to identify principles of social cooperation (or principles of justice) that have the most reasonable chance of being endorsed and enforced by the society as a whole into the future. The social demographics identified as the context of choice, supplemented with the fact of flux, establishes that a choosing subject could not know, or hope to know, where possible normative rivals will come from (beyond the obvious alternatives of immigration and group mitosis) or what norms will be the target of disagreement and possible conflict. But as we argued above, the politically salient norms that are endorsed and enforced by some cultural community will matter, and matter greatly, to those who endorse and enforce them.

Because these norms matter within these cultural communities, their protection and defense against possible intrusions from without must also matter to the people who populate these communities. While norm circles, or norm circle clusters, will have their own internal politics (thanks to the underdetermination of norms), it seems sensible to suppose that their members will also want to defend themselves against outside invasion or intrusion. Enforcing an endorsed norm means more than just passing it along to new generations; it also means protecting it against outsiders who might prefer to do away with it or supplant it with a norm of their own. Conversely, enforcing an endorsed norm may also mean practicing a form of normative imperialism by imposing and enforcing some norm on those who have thus far failed to endorse it (and for reasons discussed at the end of the previous chapter). These factors, altogether common in the history of religious and ideological conflict, help drive the normative unrest that produces the problem of pluralism.

It would seem, then, that the first and most urgent goal of peaceful coexistence with potential normative rivals is to safeguard a norm circle's internal affairs and internal politics against outside intrusion. To guarantee this, a choosing subject asked to select a principle of justice capable of securing peaceful coexistence would likely adopt a principle that guarantees that her or his norm circle(s) will be free *from* outside interference *to* live by the norms and follow the ways that matter to the members of this circle. Group affairs and group concerns, according to this principle, are to remain exclusively the business of the group, and group ways and practices secured against meddling from without. Because this principle safeguards group freedom, or the jurisdictional autonomy of the group with regard to its own internal practices, activities, and operations, we can say that it promotes and defends a right of group autonomy.

If this approximates to a first principle of civil association that any choosing subject would hit upon when asked to select principles for the governance of her or his society, then any choosing subject should also understand that all other choosing subjects would also hit upon this principle. Under the conditions of choice, the selection of a desired good (group autonomy) guarantees its universalization. Therefore, all choosing subjects—all imaginable members of the polity, regardless of the actual norm circle(s) to which they belong—will elect to defend a group right to the autonomy of their cultural communities. It follows that the principle of justice that should be accepted in order to address the problem of pluralism holds that all cultural communities should be permitted the freedom to govern, control, and pursue their internal ideals, beliefs, convictions, and practices compatible with a similar freedom for all other cultural communities present within the jurisdictional boundaries of the state (cf. Carr, 2006, pp. 83–85).

The derivation of this principle depends upon only a few basic facts about social life that indicate the natural importance of certain dimensions of culture (certain norms that matter) in individual lives. But the acceptance of the principle no doubt demands more than a mere claim about its attraction for anonymous choosing subjects armed with the requisite sociological and anthropological data. Even considered abstractly as choosing subjects, it is difficult for people to slough off the hold that their cultural norms have on them—difficult, that is, to slough off the norms that already occupy the space where norms of social justice would go and that already prefigure thinking about the subject of social justice. The true test of principles of justice, then, involves asking if their theoretical articulation captures, conveys, and promotes with appropriate precision the general normative concerns, ill-defined as they most likely are, that belong to, and partly constitute, *our* political culture.

This takes us back to the notion of freedom of conscience. In order to make the right to group autonomy more attractive as a fundamental principle of social justice, it would be good to indicate that the right merely puts formally and exactly the political good of freedom that is already acknowledged and valued roughly in terms of the freedom of conscience that Rawls supposed is "one of the fixed points of our considered judgments of justice." The general significance that religious freedom has for the Western understanding of freedom as a political good has already been thoughtfully presented by Richard Flathman, who argues that religious freedom, "so far from being limited or even special to religion, embodies the fundamental elements of the dominant modern philosophy of freedom" (1987, p. 196). But the connection between the right to group autonomy and an expanded conception of the freedom of conscience needs to be made clearer.

Freedom and cultural autonomy

There are two reasons to be suspicious of the claim that the principled defense of the right of group autonomy captures and conveys the normative spirit surrounding the freedom of conscience. First, freedom of conscience seems directed to individuals, or to the protection of individual freedom of thought and belief (Nussbaum, 2008; Greenawalt, 2006). But the right of group autonomy is concerned, not with individuals, but with social groups—norm circles sharing one or more politically salient norms or (a rose by another name) cultural communities. Second, the freedom of conscience may seem to target religious matters exclusively. From a historical point of view, this freedom is aimed specifically at religious belief, but the right of group autonomy protects social groups identifiable in terms of norm systems that can and likely will range well beyond religious concerns.

There is scant theoretical reason to conclude that either of these arguments is compelling, however. Both focus upon the historical narrative behind the freedom of conscience rather than the underlying logic that accounts for its normative importance. To appreciate this point, let us note initially that the highly individualistic understanding of the freedom of conscience on display in the first reason is premised upon a largely misleading and sadly inaccurate social ontology, as should be rather apparent given the discussion of culture in the previous chapter. Persons belong to, are socialized into, and exist within, norm circles; this is their social inheritance. It is this inheritance, in large measure, and not mere biology that makes persons into independent human beings. Nor is there much reason to take issue with the fact of human sociality at this point in the evolution of human self-understanding (cf. Christman, 2009, pp. 66–85).

The ideal of freedom always involves the protection of difference, and the difference that requires protection is invariably lodged in a very real disagreement that has political significance for the society in question. Freedom is not a political value because it protects the occasional idiosyncratic individual; it is a value because it mediates substantial normative disputes between groups of people. Once again, the Roger Williams story has enduring value.

Williams and his followers split with the elders of the Bay, as we have seen, with regard to certain crucial norms of the Puritan faith. Williams thought that Puritanism should permit everyone to inquire into the true nature of man's devotion to God and not have the theological convictions of the saints of the faith imposed upon them and enforced against them by the coercive might of the state (James, 1984, pp. 324–326). At issue were competing norms about how individuals should properly pursue and safeguard their devotion to God. But Williams did not stand alone on this matter; nor was he just a solitary crackpot whom the elders of the Bay could easily ignore. Had this been the case, he would not have posed much of a threat to their authority. But he led a group of fellow dissidents who had formed a new norm circle by endorsing and enforcing amongst themselves a revised theological (and politically salient) norm cluster. Thus a new community of individuals identifiable by virtue of a commitment to a revised norm cluster that replaced key aspects of the norms they previously accepted stood in opposition to the parent community whose leadership sought to continue to impose upon them the norms they had come to reject. In pressing for soul freedom, Williams and his followers wanted the opportunity to practice their shared religious convictions in the manner they deemed proper.

What Williams and friends wanted was a type of group autonomy—the right to practice and pursue their beliefs as they saw fit, and not to have these matters dictated to them by the saints of the faith. Williams thought his religious views were correct and proper and the views of the elders of the Bay misbegotten, and he expressed this point in terms of his defense of soul freedom. But what he and his followers wanted was to *practice* soul freedom and not be prevented from doing so by the civil authorities, who he believed had no business involving themselves in theological matters. His theology inclined him to focus upon individual conscience—the freedom to worship as one saw fit; yet this focus belies the fact that he was not really defending the conscientious beliefs of the individual. Rather, he was defending the freedom of his hearty band to live by their own religious convictions and practice their faith as they saw fit; he was defending, in short, a right of group autonomy (cf. Bozeman, 1972). In other words, the freedom Williams insisted upon protected religious communities intent upon practicing their respective faiths, and not the conscience of the solitary individual alone.

These remarks call to mind another aspect of the right to group autonomy that should be considered at this point. Suppose we recall that the Supreme Court in *Reynolds* held that the free exercise clause protects freedom of conscience but not the freedom to act upon conscientious belief. One is free, on this view, to believe whatever one wants to believe, but one is not free to act upon these beliefs if they are considered grossly objectionable by society as a whole. Interestingly, this also seems to have been the view of the elders of the Bay with regard to Roger Williams. Had Williams kept his mouth shut and clung to his principles in private, he would not have found himself in trouble with the magistracy of the Bay. But he persisted in advocating his principles "using the most powerful instrument of persuasion at that time—the pulpit," and this the elders of the Bay could not abide (Stead, 1934, p. 246).

What matters at this point is that Williams understood the advocacy of his principles to be a feature or aspect of his religious belief. Beliefs are not solely or exclusively mental states; they are rather guides to action. The belief that water is liquid, for example, is not just an epistemological insight that a person holds in the privacy of her conscience. It informs and directs the way a person will interact with water, put it to use, deal with it, and so forth. As philosophers have noticed since Aristotle, actions involve beliefs; beliefs are the things that shape the norms we act upon. It is simply not possible to parse belief from action without denigrating the belief in question. Moreover, there is no need to insist upon the freedom of belief independently of the freedom to act upon beliefs, for unless one lives in a horribly Orwellian world, outsiders cannot restrain or control a person's mental states, as Spinoza emphasized some time ago. Thus a freedom of belief parsed from the freedom of action makes no sense because restraints can only reach action, not belief. So, just as freedom is invariably concerned with the protection of difference, it is also focused upon the protection of action—of sustaining the opportunity for persons to act as they wish to act and to live by the norms that matter to them.

Consequently, the peculiar logic of the *Reynolds* decision should be rejected and recognized for what it really seems to be: a way of rationalizing what we called above the great American compromise by effectively reducing the free exercise clause to near pointlessness. Our choosing subject asked to select principles of justice to govern her or his society would almost certainly not think to endorse a principle intended to protect group autonomy and yet still hold that this principle should reach only belief and not action. A choosing subject would be attracted to the idea that the freedom of conscience protects only belief and not action only as a way to reconcile her principled commitment to the ideal of freedom with the fact that this freedom would appear to permit others to do something she considers horribly immoral, objectionable, or intolerable. But of course, this is what freedom does; if the elders of the Bay had not been scandalized by Roger Williams's temerity from the pulpit, there would have been no need for him to insist on the value of soul freedom in the first place.

This brings us to the second reason why the principle of group autonomy might seem to wander away from the notion of freedom of conscience. A right to group autonomy would protect all internal group activities from the coercive interference of outsiders, including state officials. But freedom of conscience is ordinarily associated with unhindered religious worship, and therefore, the principled defense of group autonomy might seem overbroad because it seems to reach group activities and events not associated with religious worship.

By way of response, we should note first that the specific historical locus of concern in Anglo-American politics that gave birth to freedom of conscience was the fact of religious difference, and the lingering consequence of this historical contingency is that the political defense of group autonomy is conceptually limited to religious groups. But the point of honoring the autonomy of religious communities need not, and arguably should not, be restricted to respect for religious difference alone. The historical lesson that produced a concern for religious freedom (freedom of conscience) was driven by political, and not theological, matters.

This is where the liberal defense of religious freedom parts company with Roger Williams's concern for soul freedom. For Williams, soul freedom was a theological norm, an element of the faith so to speak. But the liberal defense of religious freedom regards this commitment as a political norm, and thus one that stands independently of particular religious beliefs. As a political norm, freedom of conscience is designed to promote and protect the peaceful coexistence amongst different religious communities who would be at each other's throat if not for the political compromise involving respect for the autonomy of all religious groups. But if the norm is seen historically to protect only the autonomy of religious communities, it is because this was the only troubling source of normative difference at the time of its evolution.

In other words, public peace, political stability, and good order were and remain the goals that drive the endorsement and enforcement of this norm. It just happened that the specific historical threat to this peace, stability, and good order was produced by religious difference. But this threat to social stability and good order could just as easily have come from some other source of normative conflict that proved disruptive of social life. Regardless of the source, however, the logical remedy to this conflict would still be the same and would still counsel in favor of a liberal compromise that required respect for the autonomy of the communities in conflict. Thus the general point and spirit of the norm of freedom of conscience should not be confused with the particulars of its historical origin.

So then, it is the strategy for dealing with divisive normative conflict that resonates politically in the story of an emergent freedom of conscience, and therefore it is this strategy that should be generalized across the political landscape. It is unrealistic to expect immigrant groups to check their culture (their politically salient norm clusters) at the border, just as it is impossible to halt the dynamics of group mitosis. So to mitigate the threat of intergroup conflict, a strategy of peaceful coexistence is required, and the strategy that will certainly appeal to the informed choosers of principles of justice is on display in the historical struggle that led to the domestication of religious conflict in the West. In fact, religious conflict is simply a dimension of cultural conflict—or normative conflict—given the account of culture presented above, and this adds additional reason to conclude that a right of cultural autonomy is no great logical distance from the notion of freedom of conscience.

It seems, then, that cultural communities can be expected to value their ways and practices and to desire to live according to the norm systems that matter to them and that they endorse for, and enforce upon, their progeny. A compromise that secures for them this opportunity, and insulates them from intergroup conflict, would seem most desirable. This is what our adaptation of the Rawlsian process for the selection of principles of justice is designed to establish. And it indicates why a political system that endorsed and enforced the norm expressed by the principle of cultural autonomy would be acceptable to all elements of the polity regardless of the other (more basic and less derivative) norm clusters they happen to accept. Accordingly, we shall suppose for present purposes that this argument produces a viable resolution to the problem of pluralism and that intercultural normative conflict should be mediated, politically and legally, by recourse to the right of cultural autonomy.

Law, crime, and justice

It is now time to consider how, if at all, a right of cultural autonomy helps resolve the question about the need for a cultural defense in American criminal law. The most obvious and least interesting thing to say about this is that the legal system should be held responsible for defending and respecting the right of cultural autonomy in both its civil and criminal operation. But this really goes without saying; what we need to understand is what the officers of the legal system must do in order to meet this responsibility. Since we are concerned here exclusively with the criminal law, we shall put aside consideration of how civil law should operate in order to meet the requirement to respect group autonomy. This means the present challenge is to fill in the gap between the theoretical inquiry into fundamental principles of social justice and the nitty-gritty of practical policy proposals derived from the theoretical conclusions reached thus far. How, then, does the right of cultural autonomy help structure the operation of American criminal jurisprudence?

As a prelude to this issue, it might be good to say some things about the nature and function of modern criminal law. The development of law through history has of course been greatly influenced by customary practice. As Harold Berman has put it, "[L]aw is something that grows out of the patterns and norms of behavior, the folkways and mores, of the community" (1983, p. 82). This invites recollection of Hart's view that a legal system emerges when primary rules (action guiding norms) that have standing as customary practice within some society are formalized and reinforced with secondary rules of recognition, adjudication, and change. And it suggests that the initial authority of law is connected closely with what Berman calls the "sanctity of custom" (1983, p. 82).

The close relation between law and custom is actually displayed, and not contradicted, by the equally significant connection between law and religion, for religion was a central dimension of the customs of European peoples. As one would expect, then, the connection between crime and sin is clearly evident in the development of Western law (Berman, 1983, pp. 185–195). Together, custom and religion are crucial underlying sources of the substance of law that developed in the various Western states. But they are hardly the only sources of this substance. Lawrence Friedman has pointed out, for example, that even in the heavily theological Boston of the days of the Puritans, where "criminal codes were suffused with notions of sin, there was a heavy dose of politics and economic policy in them as well" (Friedman, 1973, p. 64).

As a cultural phenomenon, the institution of law has emerged as a mechanism for the endorsement and enforcement of certain norms thought to have a special importance within its jurisdiction. And the history of the development of law in states such as the US, that rely heavily upon the rule of law for order, prosperity, and justice, is a story of the process by which norms, considered important enough to require the status of law, came to be considered important *because* they were accorded the status of law. This is a story that involves the transformation of the normative basis of norm systems; norms that mattered because of their customary or religious significance were transformed by imposing upon them a new normative status—the status of law (Berman, 1983, p. 194). Because these norm systems defined a culture that ranged over moral, economic, and political aspects of the community, the legal system became infused with the moral, economic, and political norms of the community. These remarks will of course call the normalcy function of law back into view, for they summarize the point behind this function.

Yet the great challenge this process must face involves the development and maintenance of consistency and coherence across the range of norms that receive legal status. How does a capitalist society that values equal opportunity in life, for example, configure a legal system that reconciles an economic theory that readily produces tremendous inequality of wealth with its moral commitment to equal opportunity? And to add an additional element of complexity, any legal system that is capable of supporting political stability must be capable of managing the fact of social change, whether driven by immigration, group mitosis, or (most likely) both. In order to meet the twin challenges of complexity and change, a state will need to identify and promote certain galvanizing principles that can guide both political and legal systems in the process of addressing the problems of complexity and change produced by the problem of pluralism. A state that lacks such principles is likely to become unstable by virtue of the political conflicts that may well arise amongst the various different cultural communities whose ways and practices place them in opposition to one another.

In the case of the criminal law, the more practical side of this general problem involves making decisions about which activities and behaviors should properly be criminalized and sanctioned by means of law. What is the proper reach and limit of the normalizing function of law? Both social pluralism and social change put tremendous pressure on the belief that a common and standardized code of legal conduct can serve effectively and justly across a large and culturally (morally, religiously, ethnically, and even ideologically) diverse population. But the need for a principled solution to the question about the kind of conduct that is properly prohibited by criminal law has not gone unnoticed in Western political thought, and two generally recognized schools of thought on how best to address this problem have emerged. Both approaches should be understood to attempt a reconciliation between the normalcy and justice functions of criminal law. So, the question is simply this: Which of these two reconciliation strategies best honors the right to cultural autonomy?

The first approach is derived from and inspired by J.S. Mill's familiar harm principle introduced above:

> "the sole end for which mankind are warranted, individually or collectively, in interfering with the liberty of action of any of their number, is self-protection. That the only purpose for which power can be rightfully exercised over any member of a civilized community, against his will, is to prevent harm to others."
>
> (Mill, 1951, pp. 95–96)

Mill pressed his argument for this in reasonably libertarian fashion; his intended aim was to defend individual freedom by imposing principled limits upon the authority of the state (and hence upon the legal system of the state). But it should be readily apparent that his principle has a moral basis; the state is justified in restraining someone from harming another because it is (pro tanto) morally wrong to harm another person against her or his will. To understand the reach and substance of the criminal law, then, all we need do is fashion a general theory of harm to others of the sort carefully developed by Joel Feinberg in his masterful four-volume work, *The Moral Limits of the Criminal Law* (1984; 1985; 1986; 1990).

The difficulties that surround Mill's principle are both rather evident and quite notorious. The most familiar of these involves identifying a compelling account of what counts as harming another (cf. Feinberg, 1984). Determinations of harm are judgmental, of course, and consequently they contain a normative component. Harming, we might say and in a fashion inspired by Feinberg, involves a morally objectionable intrusion upon another's interests. But even if we could fashion a theory of harm that we would be happy to endorse as an objective moral standard, the further problem with this approach involves getting all possible cultural communities that might belong to the state to accept it. The problem of pluralism places this possibility in immediate doubt, for different norm systems may involve competing and inconsistent accounts of harm (cf. Honig, 1999, pp. 35–40). The harm principle is hard-pressed, then, to meet the litmus test of social justice—the general acceptability condition—because while it is possible that all cultural communities in the state would agree that harming others should not be allowed, they need not agree on what harming others involves, or what constitutes a setback of another's interests. Therefore, they would not agree on the actual content of the criminal law. And the imposition of one group's construction of harm on other cultural communities within the state, even if the prevailing group's standard represents a substantial majority of the population, would clearly violate the right of cultural autonomy.

The second approach to the matter of criminalization is illustrated by Lon Fuller's suggestion that law in general serves the significant social purpose of "ordering and facilitating human interaction" (1971: 198). Fuller understands this to mean that law works best when it facilitates the interaction of what he calls "friendly strangers." This view is best understood by considering the way law facilitates economic activity in capitalist economies by ordering and controlling exchanges between parties looking to enter mutually advantageous arrangements involving the exchange of recognized goods. Law provides security for these arrangements where mere trust in one's neighbor is not enough. But Fuller extends his point to criminal law by noting that this branch of law provides some assurance that people can go about their business without fear of interference from others (1971: 197).

This point is of some importance because it suggests the need to distinguish between law's initial foundation in customary practice and its general purpose. As it developed from the customs and folkways that commanded attention among certain cultural communities, law merely formalized social expectation by enabling the state to police these matters; here the customary source of law worked in perfect harmony with the purpose of law as a means of sustaining good social order, or in Fuller's terms, furnishing "base lines for human interaction" (1971: 201). The law of murder, for example, formalized a cultural taboo against the unjustified taking of human life. It did so, moreover, because murder was considered morally reprehensible, or *malum in se* (the normalizing function of law), but it also served the purpose of reinforcing a cultural norm in order to guarantee that the norm would be observed in a fashion that promoted social order and peace (the justice function of law). As Fuller points out, the law of murder put an end to the possibility of blood feud as one family sought its own retribution (or vengeance) against what its members considered a wrong done to one of their own (Fuller, 1971).

But Fuller's rather idealized account of what law should do also has a conservative element that raises difficulties for its application to a pluralist state. By formalizing customary practice, the legal system develops as a mechanism for facilitating the interaction of "friendly strangers" by addressing conflicts that arose because of questions about, or from violations of, the activities associated with this practice. The ability of law to facilitate the interaction of friendly strangers, in other words, depended, at least initially, upon the fact that a shared norm system was already in place that made this interaction possible. But the challenge produced by the problem of pluralism is that there is no initial norm system in place to make this interaction possible. The problem of pluralism is a product of the fact of cultural (normative) difference, and consequently, in order to facilitate interaction between such cultural strangers, law must be informed by political norms that all cultural communities present in the state can endorse and adopt as an aspect of their own beliefs.

Fuller's account of law encourages us to concede that law should facilitate interaction among the cultural communities present in the state, but his reliance upon customary practice in order to identify the content of criminal law is not very helpful at this point. Further, Fuller's application of the notion of friendly strangers may also seem rather out of place. If we again think back to Roger Williams and his problems with Massachusetts Bay, for example, it seems the strangers involved were not really very strange to one another, and they were certainly not the least bit friendly. But political history can again prove helpful in addressing this matter and in bolstering an account of criminal law as a vehicle for facilitating peaceful interaction throughout the state. To see this, we need only recall the lesson learned in the US, and elsewhere, about how to live with the fact of often divisive religious difference. The lesson, once again, is that religious communities should be permitted to live according to their ways and practice their beliefs as they see fit, within a system of rules (laws) that guarantee them the right to do this without fear of being oppressed or dominated by other religious communities who might take exception to their beliefs or their ways. This lesson, stated in more general terms, returns us to the right of cultural autonomy.

Government and sovereignty

If it is supposed that the right of cultural autonomy should be invoked to make decisions about what conduct the state should and should not criminalize, the conclusions that seem to follow from the above discussion would seem to be downright gloomy. The fact of normative difference in a pluralist state makes it all but impossible to imagine a common corpus of criminal prohibitions that either endorse and enforce, or remain consistent with, the various cultural communities present within the US. In fact, the discussion thus far indicates that the normalcy function of the criminal law takes on added normative significance. Particularly with the decay of other social institutions that once did more to serve a normalcy function, the law is increasingly the primary defender of the core elements of the conventional morality of the dominant culture (or dominant cultural communities) in the United States. It performs the integral cultural function of endorsing and enforcing key elements of the norm systems that are the most prevalent, and for many the most significant, within American society, and it fulfills this function primarily through the mechanisms of the criminal law.

There is also reason to supplement this point with the additional understanding that the criminal law now also serves as a primary tool for the pursuit and promotion of the certain (liberal) ideals that resonate with increasing favor across a majority of the population. Law, in this regard, looks forward as well as backward (Kymlicka, Lernestedt, & Matravers, 2014, p. 2). It endeavors to punish wrongdoers justly, but it is also used by legislatures (and perhaps at times the judiciary) to put into effect laws that promote desirable social ends, or social ends considered desirable according to the evolving norms of the dominant culture. The role of law in the long, disturbing, and continuing effort to promote racial, gender, and distributive justice in the US is clear evidence of this more remedial use of criminal law. And this pursuit of normative integrity and consistency is also an important element of the process of endorsing and enforcing norm systems that matter to those groups of persons that form the dominant culture.

This is hardly a new phenomenon in the history of American jurisprudence, of course; the law has always been implicated in the social process through which increasingly discredited norms are dis-endorsed and more favored norms embellished and more forcefully endorsed. Consider, for example, the role law has played in the elimination of slavery and the battle against racism, the struggle for gender equality, and even prohibition. But this aspect of American jurisprudence should not be associated with the justice function of law as that notion is employed here. The battle to make the ideals of the dominant culture a more exact political reality is certainly something that should be recognized as a struggle for greater justice. But this struggle can actually stand in opposition to the right of cultural autonomy. It does so, for example, when the promoters of certain norms greatly valued by their number look to law in order punish or prohibit the practices of cultural minorities in the event these practices happen to be inconsistent with the norms they seek to promote.

This advocacy function of law, which arguably pushes beyond Fuller's concern for facilitating interaction between friendly strangers, is really a dimension of the normalcy function of law. It attempts to promote a form of social homogeneity through law, though its political agenda is more radical than conservative. In either case, however, advocacy, like normalcy, remains inconsistent with the aim of peaceful coexistence central to the case for a right of cultural autonomy. And the resultant collisions frequently produce legal challenges that are met by recourse to the great American compromise. When cultural differences find their way into court, the judiciary tends to support toleration in the event the differences at issue are not overly offensive to the moral sentiments of the dominant culture. But when cultural differences are strongly offensive to the dominant culture, toleration gives way to a compelling state interest or some other more basic judicial concern. The great American compromise drips with irony, once again, largely because it is just where the commitment to toleration seems the most necessary that it is typically found to be the most lacking.

There is little reason to dwell on the evident fact that the great American compromise generally provides little support for the right of cultural autonomy. Nor is there reason to dwell further on the possibility that criminal law can carve out space for the justice function alongside its primary concern with the normalcy function. If American law is going to find a suitable policy program for respecting the right to cultural autonomy, some other strategy will be necessary. This, however, is not—and never has been—reason to abandon the justice function of law or to conclude that it should be considered as ancillary or secondary to the normalcy (or advocacy) function of law. In fact, this is just the point where it is important to remind ourselves that the demands of justice are special across the land.

The political culture of the state is fixed by the concerns of social justice. These concerns receive expression in the political norm cluster presumably shared by all citizens. Together they represent the shared political commitments that transform a collection of diverse and possibly hostile cultural communities into a unified norm circle dedicated to the standards of justice that these commitments promise. The list of norms is arguably rather short, but no less important for that reason. Prominent on the list are the rights of free speech, press, and association, the free exercise of religion, the right of political participation and the opportunity to petition government for the redress of grievances. As argued above, to this we would add the right of cultural autonomy.

In spite of the great American compromise, these "great rights," these fundamental political norms, trump the normalcy function of law when the latter comes into conflict with the former. They display a majesty and an importance that garners them a special place in American jurisprudence, and they deserve this place by virtue of their singular importance for our understanding of justice in America. They are, of course, all norms that matter when it comes to resolving the problem of pluralism, and as such they are integral to the prospects for the peaceful coexistence of the various cultural communities that make up the citizenry of the United States.

This places the general question about the desirability of introducing some form of a cultural defense into American criminal jurisprudence in its proper political (and hence legal) context. Concerns about the need for such a defense can now be articulated as follows: Is some form of a cultural defense that would be available to the members of minority cultures, but not to members of the dominant culture, warranted within the context of American criminal law in order to protect and promote the right of cultural autonomy throughout the state? If so, how would such a defense operate, and how should it be employed by the legal system consistent with the demands of social justice the state is required to respect and promote? These questions introduce the focus of the next two chapters. But of course, connecting the right of cultural autonomy with certain other cherished civil liberties hints at the direction the argument will take.

Note

1 Rawls's contributions to the subject of social justice began in 1958 with the publication of his article, "Justice as Fairness" (Rawls, 1958). Then, in 1971, his systematic theory was presented in his book, *A Theory of Justice* (Rawls, 1971).

4 Criminal defense and cultural autonomy

Thus far the argument has been concerned almost exclusively with the theoretical basis necessary for a comprehensive consideration of the cultural defense proposal. With this material in place, the next step is to establish some appreciation for the legal milieu that has produced concerns about a cultural defense in the first place. This requires a general survey of the universe of cases where an application of a criminal defense has been thought by some—mostly criminal defense attorneys, it would seem—to serve the ends of justice. This is the purpose of the present chapter. The case discussion to follow, however, is set against the theoretical discussion of the previous chapters, and this process will permit the identification of those cases in which a cultural defense would seem required by the right of cultural autonomy, as well as those cases in which this defense does not seem appropriate.

The universe of criminal cases in which a question of culture has been raised as pertinent to criminal defense is diverse, eclectic, and complex (cf. Renteln, 2004). Therefore, the first order of business is to impose an element of order on this diversity by grouping this universe of cases into three distinct categories. As will become apparent, this grouping strategy has direct implications for the way the legal system should understand the legal controversy involved. It is designed to illustrate the logically and legally distinct issues that concerns of culture introduce into criminal jurisprudence. Once categorization is complete, the cases associated with each category will be subjected to a more thorough analysis in order to identify the category or categories in which a cultural defense seems appropriate.

Some of the cases to be discussed have achieved near legendary status in the law review literature on the cultural defense, while others are rather more obscure. And while the list of cases we shall consider is fairly modest when compared with the large number of cases that raise cultural concerns, they are at least illustrative of the various kinds of problems that cultural factors have produced for the criminal courts. It should become evident that any criminal case in which a cultural factor could plausibly be introduced by the defense in response to a charge of criminal wrongdoing will fall into one of our three categories, and the nature, relevance, and viability of the cultural factor as a defense against a finding of criminal responsibility is conditional upon the category into which the case falls.

Categorization is determined by the particular nature of the controversy raised by the case, and accordingly we shall identify them as Intra-cultural controversies (Category 1), Inter-cultural controversies (Category 2), and Culturally variable controversies (Category 3), respectively. To foreshadow, in the process of the more thorough case review we shall argue that Category 1 cases should be entitled to a cultural defense if the right of cultural autonomy is to be taken seriously, but Category 2 and 3 cases should not be entitled to such a defense.

Culture and crime: a classification scheme

Category 1: Intra-cultural controversies

As the name implies, our first category is composed of cases in which a criminal controversy is generated by a state's legal involvement with, or intrusion into, the internal affairs and activities of some minority cultural community. The case of *State v. Kargar* (1996) is an apt illustration. This case involved an Afghan man who had lived in the US for roughly four years prior to his prosecution for gross sexual assault by his home state of Maine. The Maine gross sexual assault statute prohibits contact between an adult's mouth and a young boy's penis, and Kargar, who was observed on a number of occasions kissing his 18-month-old son's penis, admitted at trial that he had done this. In his defense, he noted that kissing the penis of one's child is not considered wrong, sexual, or offensive according to Afghan culture; instead, it is considered a way of expressing fondness for the child, a fact that was supported by expert testimony (*Kargar*, 1996, p. 83). Yet the Maine gross sexual assault statute did not require a showing of sexual gratification, for the Maine legislature apparently presumed that any such touching could not qualify as sexually innocent (*Kargar*, 1996, p. 85).

Kargar provides us with a case in which a person followed a cultural practice common to him and in so doing unwittingly violated a criminal statute even though the act in question was considered innocent and not criminal by the cultural community to which the person belonged. It raises the question whether Kargar should be held criminally responsible for violating a valid criminal statute even though the cultural meaning of his actions seems innocent enough, at least when viewed from within the context of his own culture. So then, what should a legal system committed to respecting the right of cultural autonomy do with Kargar?

The second case falling within our first category is *Ex parte Crow Dog* (1883). In this case, Crow Dog, a Brule Sioux, sought habeas corpus relief from his imprisonment for the crime of murder following his conviction by a Dakota territorial court. Crow Dog had killed another Brule Sioux on tribal lands and had already been convicted of the crime of murder by tribal law enforcement authorities. He argued that territorial courts lacked jurisdiction over intra-tribal affairs and that such matters were under the sole jurisdiction of tribal authorities. The Supreme Court held that jurisdiction over internal tribal affairs remained within the exclusive jurisdiction of the tribes, as a surviving attribute of tribal sovereignty, if Congress had not expressly acted to limit tribal self-government. In this particular case, the Court could not find statutory evidence that Congress had so intended to limit tribal sovereignty by claiming federal jurisdiction over crimes committed by tribal members against other tribal members on tribal land.

The *Crow Dog* decision was issued in an era when popular sentiment supposed that Native Americans should abandon their customary ways and assimilate into mainstream American culture. This likely explains why Congress responded to the decision by appending to the Appropriation Act of 1885 the Major Crimes Act that identified seven crimes over which federal courts would have jurisdiction even if they occurred on tribal lands and between tribal members. Though unusual for its time, the *Crow Dog* decision was remarkably sensitive to and accepting of the cultural differences between Native American ways and mainstream American society. Tribal punishment for Crow Dog's offense required him to support the dependents of the tribal member he had killed through payment of money, horses, and goods, but it did not subject him to the death penalty (Kingsbury & Smith, 1915, p. 1194). In the eyes of the Brule Sioux, justice was properly done by the tribal court, and that should have been an end to the matter. But because that was not an end to the matter in the eyes of the territorial authorities, the case raises the question whether the right to cultural autonomy should be understood to block further prosecution by federal courts.

The third case in this category is the much discussed *People v. Moua* (1985). Defendant Kong Moua was a Hmong tribesman from Laos. The Hmong traditionally practice arranged marriages and the parents and clans set the marital duties of their children. But the Hmong have also developed two strategies by which either a man or a couple can force the marital question, so to speak, upon their respective families and clans. One of these, known as "marriage by capture" (or *zij poj niam*) involves the abduction and rape of a woman by a man wishing to take her for a bride. The other, generally referred to as "marriage by elopement," involves a simulated kidnap and rape by a couple wishing to marry that is intended to leave the parents and clans faced with a fait accompli need to allow the marriage (Evans-Pritchard & Renteln, 1994, p. 14).

In *Moua*, the defendant believed that Seng Xiong, his intended bride, had agreed to marry him, and he believed they had elected to pursue the "marriage by elopement" practice together (Evans-Pritchard & Renteln, 1994, pp. 10, 22). At some point after events had played themselves out, Seng Xiong told a different story, claiming that she had been kidnapped by Moua and a friend of his and forced to have sexual relations with him. Following a failed effort by the families to reach a mutually acceptable settlement to the situation, Xiong called the police, and Moua was charged with the crimes of kidnap and rape. In his defense, Moua claimed he thought he and Xiong were playing out the marriage by elopement practice, although Xiong did not support this understanding of things.

The judge apparently believed both parties and held that Moua could not be convicted of the crime of rape because he was not aware that his victim was not consenting to his sexual advances. Moua eventually pleaded guilty to the reduced charge of false imprisonment and served a much lighter sentence than he might have because cultural factors were introduced to support a mistake of fact defense (Evans-Pritchard & Renteln, 1994, p. 26). *Moua* is a complicated case, and one that raises genuine concerns amongst many people within mainstream American culture about what seems to be an abusive social practice. But the case also raises equally important questions about whether the right to cultural autonomy permits the state to have any criminal interest in the internal politics of a distinctive cultural community.

The final case that we shall place in our first category is *The People v. Assad* (2010). Assad was found guilty, by a California district court, of torturing his minor son through administration of corporal punishment (*Assad*, 2010, p. 702). According to the facts detailed by the California appellate court that considered his appeal, Assad bound the child's hands and feet to a bed frame and beat him on both the front and back of his body with various objects, including a garden hose with a metal end and a wooden stake. He also bit the child, punched him in the mouth, choked him, hit him with a stick and with a spoon, and scalded the bottom of the child's foot with a knife blade he had heated for that purpose (*Assad*, 2010, pp. 703–704).

Assad introduced evidence during trial that his Syrian culture and his religion permitted the use of corporal punishment. Presumably, the introduction of this information was intended to establish that the child-rearing and disciplinary practices of his culture differed in pertinent ways from the disciplinary practices of the majority culture in the United States. Specifically, his culture placed responsibility on parents to discipline their children, and hitting children with instruments was purportedly a culturally acceptable form of punishment (*Assad*, 2010, p. 705).

On appeal, Assad asked the court to find that his case was burdened by the ineffective assistance of counsel because at trial his attorney should have submitted a pinpoint jury instruction regarding a "cultural defense," which would have instructed the jury that Assad's cultural perspective would negate the intent element necessary to have been convicted of the crimes with which he was charged (*Assad*, 2010, pp. 707–708). The court rejected this argument, holding that such an instruction would be an improper comment on the evidence, rather than an appropriate instruction (*Assad*, 2010, p. 708). *Assad* appears to resemble *Kargar* in several pertinent ways; therefore, the case raises the question whether our treatment of *Kargar* should extend to *Assad*, even though Assad's behavior is likely to seem substantially more offensive than Kargar's to members of the dominant American culture.

Category 2: Inter-cultural controversies

Our second category is well-represented by two cases. In the first, *State v. Butler* (1985), three members of the Siletz tribe living near Portland, Oregon were accused of the murder of Donald Pier. Pier had been rumored to be involved in the grave robbery of Siletz tribal burial grounds. The State of Oregon claimed that when Gary Butler, Dino Butler, and Robert Van Pelt, all members of the

Siletz tribe, heard these rumors and presumed them to be true, they went to Pier's house and stabbed him to death (Chiu, 2006, p. 1361).

The three defendants were eventually acquitted for lack of proof. The State was unable to demonstrate satisfactorily that the defendants were in fact the three individuals who took Pier's life (Renteln, 1993, p. 454; Chiu, 2006, p. 1362). But although cultural factors were not finally dispositive of the case, they raised interesting prospects for the introduction of a cultural defense. Evidence was introduced at trial indicating that, according to tribal belief, grave robbing disturbs the peace of ancestral spirits. The proper remedy is either to return the stolen artifacts to their initial place or spill the blood of the perpetrator (Chiu, 2006, p. 1363). Because the stolen artifacts were long gone by the time Pier's life was taken, it would seem that the spilling of blood was the only tribal option for restoring the peace of the ancestral spirits.

Interestingly, this cultural information can plausibly be used by the prosecution to establish a motive for the killing of Pier. But it could also be used by the defense to establish a justification for his killing if it is supposed that tribal law mandates the killing and the right of cultural autonomy entitles tribal members to follow law and tribal practice under such circumstances. Accordingly, we shall presume that the three defendants in *Butler* were sincerely acting upon the cultural belief that the only way to appease the spirits of their ancestors was to kill the grave-robber, and we shall further presume that this is what was required of them according to tribal culture. Neither presumption was challenged in court, and the latter presumption was generally considered faithful to tribal customary belief. Had Pier been a member of the tribe, he would have known that this fate would likely befall him if he happened to be discovered as a grave-robber by his fellow tribal members. But Pier was not a tribal member, and the issue raised by the case for present purposes is whether tribal jurisdiction for securing justice for the spirits of the tribal ancestors should be permitted to extend beyond tribal members according to the right of cultural autonomy.

United States v. Le (2009) is the second and final case illustrative of Category 2. Le had been a political prisoner in Vietnam, and following the war he was granted refugee status by the United States. After becoming a naturalized citizen, he traveled to Vietnam, where he met and married his wife, My Nga Ly. Ly, hoping to join her husband in the US, applied for but was denied a visa to visit the United States. Le then asked Congressman Bobby Scott for information about the denial, which Scott provided. As it turned out, the Consular Chief in Vietnam asserted that no evidence existed to establish a bona fide relationship between Le and Ly. Upon receiving this news, Le sent Congressman Scott a letter that made references to the 2007 Virginia Tech shootings and threatened to decapitate the Consular Chief in Vietnam. Le also smeared the letter with his own blood (*Le*, 2009, pp. 1–2).

These facts were uncontested by Le, who originally pleaded guilty to violating a federal statute related to mailing threatening communications (*Le*, 2009, p. 2). However, at his sentencing hearing, he sought to withdraw his initial plea of guilty. He did so because he had become convinced that he was actually innocent of the charges brought against him. He argued, in part, that his culture rendered him incapable of understanding that such a communication would be threatening. Therefore, he lacked the requisite *mens rea* to have committed the offense (*Le*, 2009, p. 9). He insisted that his cultural background inclined him to consider the letter an insult rather than a threat, and he further argued that he lacked the sufficiency in English that would have led him to understand that the letter would be construed, by members of the majority culture, as a threat (*Le*, 2009, pp. 9, 23). From his cultural perspective, the blood-smearing was "letting blood," which is a Vietnamese practice meant to vouch for the truthfulness of a document's content. Similarly, the phrase "cut his head off" was meant idiomatically as an insult—the meaning it apparently carries in Vietnamese, rather than as a threat. Le cited his lack of understanding of English and the apparent cultural differences for what he believed to be simply a big misunderstanding. The Court allowed Le to withdraw his guilty plea, but the question of Le's criminal responsibility remained in place. For present purposes, the case raises the question whether the right of cultural autonomy blocks finding Le criminally responsible for his actions once their cultural meaning is made apparent?

Category 3: Culturally variable controversies

Our final category is composed of those cases where cultural factors appear to matter to the determination of criminal responsibility in spite of the fact that the right of cultural autonomy is not relevant to them, and for reasons that need to be made clear. These cases introduce a variety of obscure, uncertain, and controversial cultural elements into the criminal justice system. Sometimes this obscurity is the product of social change, as can be illustrated by a situation where some cultural practice is no longer permitted by cultural elites even though some members of the culture may still quietly subscribe to it. At other times, norm underdetermination produces misunderstandings, or differences of viewpoint, about how some practice actually operates or what some norm really requires. In both cases, some members of cultural communities may act in a way that they believe is faithful to some cultural practice though this faithfulness to practice is disputed by others within the culture.

Category 3 cases are of this sort, though of course it is necessary to add that the defendant's actions also presumptively violate the criminal law. As should be apparent, concerns about cultural autonomy do not arise in the cases that fall within this category, but cultural variables may still matter to legal efforts to identify criminal responsibility. For this reason, culture matters in these cases, and the problem they raise is to determine how sensitivity to cultural variables can help inform an accurate finding of criminal responsibility. One way to put this is to ask whether the right of cultural autonomy entails an obligation of cultural deference in cases of this sort. Does the right of cultural autonomy require state courts to defer to cultural constructions of the extent of criminal responsibility evident in these cases?

The first case falling into this category is *People v. Kimura* (1985). This case has received considerable attention in the cultural defense literature. Fumiko Kimura attempted to commit *oya-ko-shinju*, or parent-child suicide, by walking with her children into the ocean in the Los Angeles area. She managed to kill her two children in the attempt but was prevented by rescuers from successfully taking her own life.

These actions were apparently precipitated by a series of events that began to transpire several months earlier when Kimura learned that her husband had been supporting a mistress for a number of years. Once she became aware of her husband's infidelity, she worked for several months with her husband and his mistress in an effort to find a resolution to their marital problems. Failing to realize a successful solution to the problem, she elected to deal with the shame and humiliation she felt by means of suicide. Kimura was raised in Japan and her sense of right and wrong in this matter was shaped by her Japanese culture. In customary Japanese fashion, she believed that a mother who commits suicide and leaves her children behind was a horrible person, and therefore she thought it important to take the lives of her children prior to killing herself so that they would not suffer without a mother and so that she could care for them in the afterlife.

Kimura was charged with the crime of murder for the intentional deaths of her two children. Defense counsel introduced evidence that *oya-ko-shinju* was a familiar practice in Japanese culture, and while no longer condoned or permitted by Japanese authorities, it would not receive in Japan the more severe sanctions that an American would receive for the crime of murder. Kimura's plea of voluntary manslaughter was eventually accepted by the prosecution because Kimura's actions did not seem to display the requisite *mens rea* required to establish a conviction for first degree murder. But for present purposes, the issue posed by the case is whether factors associated with Kimura's Japanese culture properly played a role in the judicial determination of what to do with her particular case. It is worth asking whether American courts should take notice of the fact that Kimura acted upon a traditional Japanese norm even though it is no longer *officially* endorsed and enforced within her native culture.

The second case we wish to consider under this category is *People v. Chen* (1989). In this case, Dong Lu Chen's wife admitted to him that she was having an affair. When Chen learned of this, he became enraged, grabbed a hammer, and hit her in the head eight times, causing her death. Chen, who had been in the US for about a year prior to this, admitted to killing his wife. At trial, the defense introduced evidence about the way divorce and infidelity are regarded in China. Chen's attorney produced evidence to show that in China a wife's infidelity is evidence of her husband's weak character and also that divorce is considered a practice that brings shame to one's family. Chen's defense was designed to establish that, because of these beliefs, it is possible that a Chinese husband who learns of his wife's infidelity may lose control of his emotions, react violently, and endanger his wife as a result.

Chen thus asserted a diminished capacity defense against the charge of murder. The trial court in Brooklyn agreed and found Chen guilty of the substantially reduced charge of second-degree manslaughter. The trial judge concluded that Chen's violence was an emotional reaction inspired to a large degree by Chinese "values about adultery and loss of manhood." Apparently, the trial judge in the case was particularly sensitive to the cultural information introduced and to the prospect that cultural factors could elicit a remarkably violent reaction from Chinese husbands upon learning of a wife's infidelity. For present purposes, the case raises the question whether this conclusion is warranted given the cultural information that was before the judge. But interest in this case should not be restricted to this matter alone. The case also generates questions about the ability of American criminal courts to understand how cultural factors influence or shape individual actions. This is relevant, in turn, to how cultural variables should properly be employed in the process of criminal defense in cases that do not involve concerns about the right to cultural autonomy.

The third case we shall place into Category 3 is *People v. Wu* (1991). In this case, Helen Wu, a Chinese native, came to the US to marry Gary Wu, with whom she had had a son several years earlier. Shortly after their marriage, the son informed his mother not only that his father had treated him badly, but also that the father was romantically connected to another woman. At that point Helen Wu, apparently distraught over the news of the poor treatment of her child and her husband's infidelity, killed her son and then attempted to kill herself. She was prevented by her husband from completing her suicide, however, and eventually was charged with the crime of murdering her son. During Wu's trial, an expert testified that in Asian culture a mother who commits suicide and leaves her children behind is considered to be irresponsible. Therefore, the expert concluded, Wu would naturally think to kill her child before ending her own life.

The question of law that sent *Wu* to the California Court of Appeals involved the trial court's failure to instruct the jury on the significance of the defendant's cultural background and its relevance to the case. The appellate court held that cultural factors were relevant to a determination of the defendant's mental state at the time she killed her son. Wu, like Chen and Kimura, appealed to cultural factors in order to support a diminished capacity defense, and this seems fairly typical of the way defense attorneys attempt to use cultural difference in criminal proceedings. The claim is that cultural background caused the defendant in each case to suffer a decline in either cognitive or volitional ability, and the resultant diminished capacity should excuse or mitigate the consequences of their evidently criminal behavior. It remains to be seen, however, whether (and if so, when) this application of cultural desiderata is appropriate for the circumstances associated with these apparently rather similar cases.

Category 1: Intra-cultural controversies

The various problems associated with Category 3 cases will be explored in the final chapter. These cases are outliers in our analysis because they do not raise direct concerns associated with the right of cultural autonomy. Because of this, they do not qualify for a cultural defense as that notion is developed and defended here. Nonetheless, cultural factors do appear to be relevant to a finding of criminal responsibility in these cases, and we might again ask whether the right to cultural autonomy might require something like an obligation of cultural deference when American courts work to measure criminal responsibility in such cases.

It is time now, however, to turn to our first two categories and consider more thoroughly the cases belonging to each. It should be apparent that the cases in Category 1 are appropriate targets for a cultural defense, and for reasons that should become clear once these cases are analyzed. Similarly, it should also become evident that Category 2 cases are beyond the reach of a cultural defense, and again for reasons that will become clear once they have been examined. With these conclusions in place, the chapter to follow will consider the legal foundations and justification for supporting a cultural defense in Category 1 cases.

Kargar: Innocence and cultural practice

Of the several cases belonging to Category 1, *Kargar* might seem to be the most sympathetic target for some kind of cultural defense. In *Kargar*, the Maine Supreme Court concluded that the Maine *de minimis* statute applied to the case because the legislature could not have imagined the possibility that the touching it wished to prohibit could actually be sexually innocent. Cultural information about Kargar's conduct made it clear that his actions were considered sexually innocent within Afghan culture, and thus such actions fell outside the range of conduct the legislators intended to sanction by means of criminalization (*Kargar*, 1996, p. 84; Wanderer & Connors, 1999, p. 838).

Because Kargar was able to establish that the meaning of his actions should be understood within their proper (Afghan) cultural context, they were rendered inoffensive in the eyes of the justices of the Maine Supreme Court. The justices could bring themselves to see Kargar's actions as a display of affection, rather than the conduct of a pedophile, and conclude accordingly that this was not the sort of thing the Maine legislature endeavored to criminalize. This outcome will no doubt seem satisfactory to anyone who is able or inclined to join the Maine Supreme Court justices in finding Kargar's actions innocent enough and their cultural explanation convincing (cf. Wanderer & Connors, 1999, pp. 842–846). Why, then, is it necessary to worry about a cultural defense under these circumstances?

The worry can be justified, however, if the circumstances differed somewhat and the justices of the Maine Supreme Court were unable or unwilling to see the practice in question as morally (and thus legally) innocent. There is some reason to think this matter should not be left to judicial discretion because the proper meaning of Kargar's actions is embedded within Afghan culture. If Afghan culture regards the practice as innocent and acceptable, then there is little reason for cultural outsiders to question or challenge this view.[1] In the absence of a cultural defense that would mandate legal toleration of an endorsed cultural practice (and the norms that power it), *Kargar* merely displays the great American compromise at work. Practices that judges can recognize or accept as morally innocuous or reasonably inoffensive are tolerated; more offensive practices—or practices regarded as more offensive according to the standards of the dominant culture—are not.

Suppose, for example, *Kargar* is compared with the events present in *Reynolds v. U.S.* (1879). *Reynolds*, it will be recalled, involved the Mormon practice of polygamy, and while the Mormon community could insist that this practice was a norm strongly endorsed and enforced by its members—and thus qualified as an element of the norm system associated with Mormon culture and the Mormon religion—it seems evident that this insistence would not have moved the justices on the Supreme Court at this particular period in time. And it would not have done so *because* the moral perspective of the justices, a perspective ensconced firmly within the norm system endorsed and enforced by the majority of Americans, inclined them to regard polygamy as morally repugnant, a view not altered by the fact that the Mormon community presumably considered this practice morally acceptable.

The moral sensitivities of the majority culture, in other words, seem dispositive of both cases. Kargar's conduct could be filtered through the prism of his own culture largely because the conduct at issue did not reach the level of moral repugnance *within the perspective of the majority culture* that was reached by the Mormon practice of polygamy. This situation is both indicative and symptomatic of the great American compromise. This compromise indicates, once again, that the judicial decision to tolerate the cultural or religious practices of minority groups hangs ultimately on how offensive these practices are considered to be when measured by the normative perspective that is dominant within the general population. Yet, this shows little respect for the right of cultural autonomy, for as we have noted previously, it is where the dominant culture is offended by some minority cultural practice that having such a right matters most. Otherwise there is little for the right to protect.

In *Kargar*, the great American compromise clearly favored the side of toleration, while in *Reynolds* things went in the other direction. But the *Kargar* decision could have gone in the other direction as well, and would most likely have done so if the cultural practice at issue had been more offensive to the normative perspective of the dominant culture. So there is reason to ask whether this legal scenario is sufficiently protective of Kargar's right to cultural autonomy, and it rather obviously is not, for the right never factors into the legal controversy. The remedy we wish to propose involves imagining a role for a cultural defense in the case that would allow the right to cultural autonomy to play a significant, if not determining, role. The defense imagined would permit the defense in a criminal proceeding to invoke the right of cultural autonomy in order to block the state from prosecuting individuals belonging to minority cultures when the conduct deemed objectionable by the state involves participation in a recognized and accepted cultural practice.

In defense of this view, let us ask initially why Maine should want to pursue a criminal prosecution of Kargar for the fact that he kissed his son's penis. Presumably, the Maine gross sexual assault statute is intended to protect children against sexual predation, and Kargar's conduct suggested to someone that child abuse was in evidence here. The state, in effect, was enforcing certain norms of the majority culture that regulate sexual activity between (culturally identified) adults and (culturally identified) minors. Kargar defended himself by pointing out that according to Afghan culture his actions were not the least bit sexual and really displayed only affection for his son. His actions were embedded in a norm system that established them as rather commonplace and inoffensive within his own culture. But the Maine justices could have seen things differently. If the Maine legislature did suppose that any touching between an adult's mouth and a young boy's penis is invariably sexual in nature, and thus properly prohibited, the justices of the Maine Supreme Court could easily have deferred to this view.

But, if Kargar has a right to cultural autonomy, this right should be fully protective of such actions without any further need to rely upon the discretion of the judiciary. The crucial issue is to decide how to build this right into criminal procedure. One way to do this is to hold the judiciary responsible for seeing the culturally charged events of a given case in the fashion at home in the minority culture presently before the bar. This is basically what happened in *Kargar*, though of course the Maine justices were not legally obligated to see things this way. But this strategy asks a great deal of judges and leaves open the possibility of slipping back toward the great American compromise.

A stronger defense of cultural autonomy would involve holding that *if* a defendant's actions belong to and follow from the defendant's adherence to valid and accepted norms of her or his cultural community, and *if* these actions affect only fellow members of the defendant's culture, then the right of cultural autonomy bars criminal prosecution for these actions in state court. And we may plausibly think of this as a cultural defense. The defense would protect the internal practices of cultural communities against criminal prosecution *regardless* of any moral criticism or condemnation aimed at them by those holding more socially dominant normative perspectives.

It is perhaps worth noting that Afghan children would not be bereft of state protection against sexual predation if this defense were acknowledged in American criminal jurisprudence. Testimony in *Kargar* made it clear that "pursuant to Islamic law any sexual activity between an adult and a child results in the death penalty for the adult" (*Kargar* 1996: 83). If the Afghan community does not police this cultural norm itself, it can hardly complain if the state polices overlapping norms belonging to the dominant culture within the Afghan community.

Crow Dog: Internal cultural jurisdiction

This brings us to *Ex parte Crow Dog*, our second Category 1 case. *Crow Dog* presents us with a curious tale in which the defendant Crow Dog was charged with the crime of murder by both his native tribe, the Brule Sioux, and by the federal government. Crow Dog's alleged criminal conduct was committed against another member of his tribe on tribal land, and his tribe had its own code of criminal conduct and its own criminal justice system that was responsible for adjudicating questions of criminal wrongdoing and punishing those found criminally liable according to tribal custom. As it happened, the punishment administered to Crow Dog by his tribe—caring for life for the dependents of the deceased—differed from his expected punishment if he had been tried in federal court. This difference mattered to some federal agents who thought the apparently lighter sentence Crow Dog received from his tribe meant that he had, in a sense, gotten away with murder. So, Crow Dog was also hauled into the Dakota territorial court, charged with and convicted of the crime of murder, and sentenced to death.

Crow Dog argued before the US Supreme Court that the territorial court lacked jurisdiction over cases involving Native Americans that occurred on tribal lands, and the Court accepted his argument at least to the extent that it held that tribal authority over Native American affairs remains within tribal jurisdiction provided that Congress does not explicitly override this jurisdiction. *Crow Dog* is admittedly unusual because it involves a distinct cultural community with its own formal legal system and a system of action guiding norms that are recognized to carry the force of law within that community. But it is not unusual for cultural communities to have some mechanisms in place for the adjudication of disputes that arise within them. Consequently, the general question that emerges from *Crow Dog* is whether these mechanisms, no matter how formal or informal they might be, should be allowed sole jurisdiction over intra-community affairs and disputes, or whether the criminal law of the state trumps this jurisdiction when some action undertaken by the members of a minority cultural community offends the law of the majority culture that surrounds it. At issue, in other words, is a question of jurisdiction: Do minority groups have the right to enforce their own norm systems and punish members who have violated cultural norms to the exclusion of prosecution by the state; or does the state have jurisdiction over such matters when the conduct at issue also involves the violation of a criminal statute?

The question, of course, has an important historical pedigree. A claim of exclusive legal jurisdiction within some territory was, and remains, an integral feature of the emergence of state sovereignty in the West. But the analysis to follow should not be understood to question or challenge this sovereign prerogative. The question that matters is whether the US should hold, as a legal matter, that minority cultures with their own judicial apparatus in place should have the right to police their own criminal affairs, even in the event of overlap with the criminal concerns of the state. A legal decision that such a right exists, by virtue of the obligation to respect cultural autonomy, is not an abdication of sovereign authority; rather, it involves an exercise of this authority.

Turning back to the specifics of *Crow Dog*, the conclusions reached in the discussion of *Kargar* would seem to recommend permitting the cultural community exclusive control of its own internal affairs, provided of course that it was able and willing to exercise this control. In *Kargar*, the defendant was accused of violating a statute that was sufficiently broad to include some conduct not considered offensive by his cultural community. His actions were not considered criminal by his community even though the statute, on its face, would invite a different conclusion. In *Crow Dog*, on the other hand, Crow Dog's conduct violated both federal law and the law of his tribe, and both jurisdictions had reason to believe that Crow Dog had committed the crime of murder. The issue that separated the legal approach of the Sioux from the federal approach involved the proper punishment for someone guilty of this crime. So, the issue raised by *Crow Dog* is whether an act considered criminal by both a minority culture and the majority culture is subject to judgments of criminal liability primarily or exclusively at home in the majority culture.

The accepted legal position on this issue, of course, is that the federal government can claim jurisdiction over putatively criminal conduct that takes place between Native Americans on tribal land if it elects to do so, but this looks a bit like conqueror's justice. And it may actually be conqueror's justice if it happens that the right of cultural autonomy establishes that minority cultures should have jurisdiction over their own internal affairs when and if they so choose. It is tempting to reject this possibility outright because Crow Dog lived within the jurisdictional parameters of the federal government and federal law is the supreme law of the land. To this we might add that the supreme law of the land is law for everyone, and accordingly, everyone should follow it and be subject to it. Lesser legal systems must yield to supreme law when a conflict of laws arises.

This response is consistent with the Supreme Court's decision in *Crow Dog*, for the Court found merely that the territorial court lacked jurisdiction in this case because Congress had not elected to exercise its sovereign authority over intra-tribal disputes at the time *Crow Dog* reached the federal bar (*Crow Dog*, 1883). It is also entirely compelling and incontrovertible; all citizens stand under a legal obligation to honor the supreme law of the land that trumps all obligations they might have to lesser legal obligations. But this point does not resolve the matter at hand, because what we really want to know is what the supreme law of the land requires with regard to jurisdictional conflicts of this sort.

There are two possibilities. First, it could mean that the sovereign authority of Congress, an authority presumably bestowed upon Congress by the Constitution, is not just supreme but also absolute; Congress is authorized to make law as it sees fit and to impose the law it makes upon all subjects of the federal government. Accordingly, Article III courts would then be authorized to exercise jurisdictional control over all disputes arising under this body of law. This, or something like it, appears to be the position of the Supreme Court in *Crow Dog*, at least with regard to congressional authority over Native Americans. Second, it could mean that the authority of Congress to use its law-making powers to regulate social life within the jurisdictional parameters of the Constitution is not absolute and that Congress is legally (that is, constitutionally) disempowered from the legal regulation of some aspects of the lives of some of the cultural communities existing within its jurisdiction.

It is arguably the second possibility that best illustrates the nature of American jurisprudence. This is most obviously evident in the case of religious liberty, but the principle of social justice that underlies the case for religious liberty, and supports the right of cultural autonomy, suggests that limitations on the authority of the federal government to regulate the affairs of minority cultures need not, and presumably should not, end with the defense of religious freedom. The right of cultural autonomy guarantees that one lot of people will not be permitted to impose its ways, practices, and beliefs on another lot of people, regardless of the moral confidence that inspires it to do so. This, we argued above, is the most compelling and stable possible resolution to the problem of pluralism. Why, then, should the federal government be entitled to try Crow Dog in federal court for the crime of murder when his offense occurred on tribal land and involved a fellow member of his tribe? The Supreme Court's claim that Congress had yet to authorize prosecutions of this sort is clearly too tepid to answer this question satisfactorily, for what we want to know is whether the legislative reach of the majority culture is properly understood to extend to situations of this sort—that is, to cases entirely internal to some cultural community with its own legal system in place to handle such matters.

Posing a question about the state's interest in claiming jurisdiction over such matters produces a familiar issue. Presumably, the state's interest here generally involves the pursuit of justice, but this notion has a double meaning in this context. On the one hand, it involves the pursuit of social justice, which would require the defense of the right of cultural autonomy (the justice function); and on the other hand, it involves enforcing and promoting the basic action-guiding norms of the majority culture (the normalcy function). These two aims come into conflict if it happens that the enforcement of the basic action-guiding norms of the majority culture permits elements of this culture to impose their ways upon minority or satellite cultures existing within the jurisdictional parameters of the state. But as should be apparent, this conflict defaults in favor of the norms of social justice in the event they are regarded as more fundamental than the majority culture's action-guiding norms.

If the norms of social justice are more fundamental in this way, it would follow that the jurisdictional authority of the state would not reach purely intra-cultural matters because the right of cultural autonomy qualifies as a norm of social justice. We will argue in the following chapter that the norms of social justice do trump state enforcement of action-guiding norms. If this is right, minority communities should be entitled to police and enforce their own basic action-guiding norms as they see fit, if they elect to do so. The mechanisms in place for this sort of thing may be more or less formal, of course, but the lack of formal adjudication procedures of the sort that happened to be evident in *Crow Dog* does not entitle the government to take jurisdiction of intra-group controversies. Cultural communities will almost certainly have developed their own internal mechanisms for sustaining and defending their action-guiding norms, for this is an essential feature of the general process by which norm systems are endorsed and enforced, and if and when some cultural community claims jurisdiction over some internal controversy, the matter is no longer the business of the government. The notable exception, of course, is the majority culture, for here government is charged with the ancillary function of being the policing agent that officially enforces the norms of this cultural community.

Moua: Internal cultural politics

This brings us to our third Category 1 case, *People v. Moua* (1985). On its face, this complicated case might seem to present an exception to the general claim that the right of cultural autonomy permits cultural communities to have jurisdiction over internal disputes if their members so wish. This would seem to be a possibility, for example, if the individual wronged by another's possibly criminal actions elects to involve the state by calling the police and alleging criminal wrongdoing. This is what transpired in *Moua*, and the call drew the Fresno, California criminal justice system into the midst of an intra-cultural conflict muddied by confusion, possible inter-cultural misunderstanding, hidden motives, and the internal politics of the Hmong.

The devil, in this much discussed case, is in the details, and the details are anything but clear. Our discussion will follow the factual account of the events of the case presented by Deirdre Evans-Pritchard and Alison Dundes Renteln in their article, "The Interpretation and Distortion of Culture: A Hmong 'Marriage by Capture' Case in Fresno, California" (1994). Apparently, the Hmong (a Southeast Asian tribe that immigrated to the US following the Vietnam War) have several ritual practices that can lead to marriage in a fashion that circumvents the usual Hmong practice of family and clan arranged marriages. Two of these are pertinent to the *Moua* case.

The first, called "marriage by capture" or "marriage by abduction" (*zij poj niam*), involves the kidnapping and "rape" of a woman by a man in search of a wife.[2] The kidnap and rape forces the family and clan of the woman to enter marriage negotiations with the family and clan of the man, but it does not necessarily result in marriage. Marriage is the outcome only if the families and clans of the principals involved reach an agreement that makes the marriage possible (Evans-Pritchard & Renteln, 1994, p. 14). Evans-Pritchard and Renteln claim that "marriage by capture" is actually rather uncommon amongst the Hmong, though it is difficult to ascertain how the practice might have changed in the US following the Hmong immigration. It seems, however, to be, or to have become, highly controversial within the Hmong community now present in the US, and it is far from clear that it constitutes a social practice premised upon norms that are widely and openly endorsed and enforced by the Hmong.

The second marriage ritual relevant to the case, called "marriage by elopement," involves an effort to circumvent parental opposition by some couple wishing to marry. This is done by staging what appears to be the kidnap and rape of the woman by the man she wishes to marry. While the details of these two practices appear to be rather similar, the "marriage by elopement" process presumes that the couple involved wish to marry one another and pursue the elopement process in order to force the hand of dissenting parents (Evans-Pritchard & Renteln, 1994, pp. 14–15). In "marriage by elopement" the woman consents to the arrangement, while in "marriage by capture" she does not. But marriage is not an automatic outcome of this practice either, for once again the marriage needs to be negotiated by the families and clans involved, and possible marriage will be sanctioned or blocked as a result of this negotiation.

The *Moua* case is often presumed to trouble because it involves the unsavory "marriage by capture" ritual (cf. Lee, 2007, pp. 954–956; Kim, 2006, pp. 209–211). Evans-Pritchard and Renteln, however, are inclined to think that the case actually involves the "marriage by elopement" ritual. From what we can tell, however, neither conclusion is really warranted. This much seems clear, Kong Moua was charged with kidnap and rape after Seng Xiong, the Hmong woman he apparently thought he was marrying, called the police and reported events that led to the filing of the charges just mentioned. According to Moua's account of what transpired, he and Xiong had agreed to marry, but sensing that Xiong's parents would not permit the marriage, he concluded that the elopement option was the best way to proceed. He thought Xiong agreed with this, and the elopement took place on April 24, 1984 (Evans-Pritchard & Renteln, 1994, p. 10).

After the elopement had taken place and Xiong had been reunited with her mother, she told a substantially different story. She claimed that she was in fact kidnapped by Moua and one of his friends, taken to Moua's house, denied the opportunity to speak with her parents, and eventually forced to have sex with Moua (Evans-Pritchard & Renteln, 1994, p. 12). She also indicated that, while she had met Moua previously and they had become friends, they were not romantically involved. So, the issue of whether the case illustrates a failed "marriage by capture" attempt on Moua's part, or a failed "marriage by elopement" collaboration between Moua and Xiong, rather depends upon whom one decides to believe. On Moua's view, the two planned a marriage by elopement but things went wrong, and Moua conjectured that this was because Xiong's mother was opposed to the marriage (Evans-Pritchard & Renteln, 1994, p. 11). But on Xiong's account, she was kidnapped and had no interest in marrying Moua at any earlier time.

Following Hmong tradition, the two families and respective clans were called upon to resolve the dispute, but no settlement was reached (Evans-Pritchard & Renteln, 1994, p. 17). Therefore, no marriage was arranged. Had all this transpired in the tribe's homeland, this would in all probability have been an end to the matter. But it was hardly the end of things for Kong Moua. After the failed negotiations, Xiong called the police to report her account of what had transpired. She claimed she called the police because she was concerned that Moua would kidnap her again. But it remains unclear why she was concerned about this. Once the marriage negotiations had collapsed, Moua had no further reason to bother Xiong since a repeat of his previous actions would still not result in marriage.

At trial, the defense combined the traditional mistake of fact defense with pertinent cultural factors. The claim was that Moua genuinely believed he was involved in the "marriage by elopement" practice with Xiong, and although he was in error about this, the mistake of fact would still defend against the charges of kidnap and rape. The judge in this case ultimately accepted a guilty plea from Moua for the much reduced charge of misdemeanor false imprisonment because he believed that Moua genuinely thought he was practicing "marriage by elopement" although he also concluded that Xiong was not really involved in this practice. While this proved to be an efficient way to dispose of the case, the interpretation of events it requires is hardly believable. It supposes, first, that Xiong's account of events is accurate; that is, it supposes Xiong was not lying and that she actually was kidnapped and raped by Moua. Second, it also supposes that Moua was wrong about his interpretation of events but that he was not lying.

The reason it seems difficult to accept this scenario involves understanding why Moua would think he was engaging in "marriage by elopement" with Xiong when, according to Hmong practice, he could also have pursued "marriage by capture" as a marriage strategy. The only reason for Moua to claim he was practicing "marriage by elopement" after the fact, and even though he was not doing so, would be to defeat the charges of kidnap and rape. And if he was genuinely practicing "marriage by elopement," it is hard to believe he could have been so certain that Xiong was a voluntary participant in the process without some fairly evident indications of consent on her part. So it is difficult to accept the view that both parties were truthfully reporting their understanding of the events that transpired between them.

But there is little reason to take a stand on this matter here, for the issue of concern at the moment is how a cultural defense might fit into this case. The defense described thus far protects minority cultures against the state's use of the criminal justice system to intrude into their practices and activities, where such intrusions are precipitated by the fact that the dominant culture holds the norm(s) that inclines its members to find the practices in question deeply objectionable. Underlying the case that supports this defense is the presumption that minority cultures may wish to manage their own internal affairs, and practice their ways as they see fit, free from the interference of more dominant social forces. But *Moua* does not clearly fit this scenario because in this case a member of the Hmong community has reached out to the state to complain that she has been the victim of criminal behavior by another member of her community.

Like *Crow Dog*, the community involved has its own dispute resolution system and internal authorities designed to address its internal problems and affairs. But unlike *Crow Dog*, where the Brule Sioux shared with the territorial government norms prohibiting murder, the criminal wrong alleged in *Moua* was apparently not also the same sort of wrong within Hmong culture. Hmong norms do not support understanding Moua's conduct in terms of rape, for rape is understood differently by the Hmong. And this indicates the oddity that haunts the case. The failed marriage negotiations between the families and clans of Moua and Xiong meant that neither side received what they wanted from the situation. The Hmong dispute resolution system did not function in a manner acceptable to either side. So, the problem posed by the case is whether Moua should be held criminally responsible for actions not considered wrong—or at least wrong in the same sense that these actions have within the dominant culture—within his own cultural community.

An affirmative answer to this question suggests the possible need to reconsider the conclusions reached in the discussion of *Kargar*. Kargar's actions did not constitute gross sexual assault within his own culture. But if that is reason to exonerate him of the charge, then it should exonerate Moua also, for his actions did not constitute rape or kidnap, as the dominant culture understands these notions, within his own culture. Imagine, for the moment, that a third party belonging to the dominant culture witnessed Moua's actions and called the police. If the police then elected to prosecute Moua for kidnap and rape, ostensibly unaware of the cultural practice in which Moua (and perhaps also Xiong) was engaged, then the case would mirror *Kargar* in all relevant respects. So, if Kargar should be permitted the use of a cultural defense, Moua should be as well.

But *Moua* is not like *Kargar* because Xiong elected to step outside the jurisdiction of her own cultural community and involve the authorities of the state. So then, does this fact alter the propriety of applying a cultural defense to this case? We might wonder at this point why a fellow member of one's own community would do such a thing. This matter troubles because it looks as if a fellow Hmong would not think that Moua had done anything wrong, or at least that he had not done the wrong the state will accuse him of doing because this wrong does not appear to exist for the Hmong. At this point several possibilities present themselves.

First, Xiong's actions could have been driven by vindictiveness. On this scenario, we should think that she (or her mother who lurks in the background of the story) became upset with the failed negotiations that would have settled the matter between the two parties and hoped to get even with Moua as best she could. On this view, the State of California provided her with a strategy for striking back at Moua and perhaps saving a bit of face within her own community. Second, she could have been upset with the Hmong norm system that regulates marital practices and hoped to drive some cultural change that would produce what she presumed to be better treatment of marriage-eligible Hmong women. On this view, we are to believe that she wanted, in effect, to politicize Hmong marital practices in order to encourage the community to revise the norms it endorses and enforces in this area. Third, she could have already split with the Hmong community on this issue and elected to endorse and enforce amongst her new norm circle different norms governing proper marital practices. If Xiong had made this move, she would no longer be traditional Hmong, and would have split with her parent culture and integrated into the dominant culture (most likely) in order to practice different marital rituals and endorse and enforce different norms. On this view, the state would be there to protect her from the members of the parent community she has elected to abandon in favor a different norm cluster.

The first two of these possibilities do not establish the impropriety of a cultural defense used to defeat a finding of criminal responsibility in the case. Vindictiveness is hardly a reason to conclude that a person should be held criminally responsible for violating the norms of a culture that is foreign to him in spite of the fact that he has not apparently violated any norms belonging to his own cultural community. There is, in any event, no apparent indication in the literature surveyed to the effect that Moua was thought by his fellow Hmong to have behaved badly or wrongly. (However, some Hmong might have had objections to his behavior *if* his actions are presumed to involve "marriage by capture" because Hmong endorsement of this practice does seem to be subject to question within the community.)

And while the surrounding cultural communities holding differing marital norms may applaud Xiong's political initiatives in the second instance, the presumption that support for her political objective justifies using the criminal justice system to coercively encourage the desired changes again illustrates the very thing the cultural defense is intended to protect against. Internal group politics should remain the private affair of the groups themselves, for what could matter more to cultural autonomy than the opportunity to settle internal political disputes as the members of some cultural community see fit. Failing a satisfactory resolution to internal political conflicts, unhappy or dissatisfied parties, either individually or collectively, may leave the group, thus giving rise to yet another example of group mitosis. But taking matters outside the cultural community in the event one is unhappy with the community's dispute resolution process is presumably something that the community as a whole would find objectionable. If this seems right, then employing a cultural defense to defeat the unwanted interference by the state in internal community affairs seems to follow as a matter of course from the right of cultural autonomy.

The right of exit introduced in the previous paragraph takes center stage in the third possible explanation of Xiong's decision to implicate the state in her dealings with Moua. Exit takes place at the time that a person shifts or alters her normative convictions and breaks with the norm cluster that is endorsed and enforced by the old norm circle. The Hmong, to repeat the lessons of the second chapter, are Hmong because they hold a cluster of politically salient norms and endorse and enforce them at least amongst themselves. A personal decision, inspired perhaps by intersectionality, to alter one's commitments and revise one's normative convictions is itself an act of exit from one's parent community. A person who rejects the norm cluster that identifies a person as Hmong is no longer Hmong. Exit, in other words, has taken place, and therefore, one has a right of physical separation that is protected by the right of exit.

It is helpful, needless to say, to advertise the fact of exit and indicate to one's parent community that one now endorses and enforces different norms regarding marital and perhaps inter-gender matters. But if exit has taken place, then Xiong's decision to enlist the help of the state to protect her against Moua is entirely understandable and legitimate. Here the right of cultural autonomy would not support the use of a cultural defense to answer charges of kidnap and rape. But as we shall see momentarily, this is because the imagined circumstances have changed the nature of the case. It now becomes an inter-cultural issue rather than an internal cultural matter, and so, if this third scenario best describes what transpired between Moua and Xiong, the case should be placed into Category 2 and removed from Category 1.

We leave *Moua* in Category 1, however, because there is no clear indication that Xiong had revised her normative convictions and elected to part company with the Hmong, or at least those Hmong who persist in practicing "marriage by elopement." The case does illustrate, however, how messy internal community affairs can become, and how complicated matters can get when distinct cultural communities collide. It is hard to see that state authorities could do much to bring a satisfactory resolution to this matter, particularly since the Hmong seemed unable to manage this using their own traditions and customary dispute resolution practices. Sometimes family feuds are best left to play themselves out, and perhaps the same can be said for minority culture feuds as well.

Assad: Intra-cultural abuse

The last case to be discussed under Category 1 is *People v. Assad* (2010). Assad was convicted of, among other things, torturing his minor son. He tied his son to a bed frame, and beat him on both sides of his body with a garden hose and a wooden stake. He also bit the child, choked him, and scalded the bottom of one of his feet with a heated knife. Assad defended himself by claiming that his Syrian culture and his faith permit the use of corporal punishment to discipline children, a claim that received rather vague and general support from one of his daughters and a relative (*Assad*, 2010, p. 193). Following his conviction, Assad claimed on appeal that, among other things, his attorney failed to request a jury instruction that would have pinpointed the different punishment techniques available to parents in Syria, thus placing his conduct in their proper cultural context and ostensibly justifying his actions (*Assad*, 2010, p. 197). The California Court of Appeals rejected this argument on the ground that such an instruction would constitute an impermissible comment on the evidence of the case (*Assad*, 2010, p. 198).

There are obvious superficial similarities between *Assad* and *Kargar*. Both involve a concern on the part of the state for the parental mistreatment of a child, and both involve a claim that the defendant was acting according to recognized cultural norms. According to the view defended here, this is sufficient to warrant the exercise of a cultural defense on the ground that conduct sanctioned or necessitated by the norm system of one's culture is placed beyond the reach of state prosecution by the right of cultural autonomy. But *Assad* differs from *Kargar* in at least one crucial respect. Assad's claim that his Islamic faith, and Syrian culture, both allow the parental use of different punishment techniques from those at home in the majority culture may in fact be quite true, but the evidence presented at trial, and as reported in the appellate decision, does little to support it (cf. *Assad*, 2010, p. 193). And even if the claim is true, it hardly follows that Assad's abusive treatment of his son would be acceptable for this reason within his Syrian culture.

These concerns would not disallow Assad's use of a cultural defense, for the right of cultural autonomy should permit this defense in cases such as *Kargar* and *Assad*. But the availability of the defense does not mean that its application will succeed. The defense, as construed here, protects intra-cultural practices and activities against state interference. Put in the most general terms, the defense would defend against efforts by the dominant culture to use the coercive mechanisms of the state to block the practice—or punish those who engage in the practice—of some minority cultural community (as defined in Chapter 2) because the practice is considered by elements of the dominant culture to be objectionable or intolerable. But the exercise of this defense will naturally require that the defendant provide compelling evidence to establish that the conduct in question really is based upon recognized cultural norms and really does fall within the parameters of an acknowledged practice of the defendant's culture.

Kargar met this requirement, and while the cultural details in *Moua* are somewhat obscure, our discussion of that case followed an interpretation of Hmong practice that met this requirement as well. No such uncertainty surrounds *Assad*, however, for in this case it is hardly clear from the available evidence that the standard was met. Moreover, from what we can tell, it would seem that Assad's attorney made very little effort to satisfy this standard. In the absence of expert testimony to the contrary, there is no reason to believe that Syrian culture, or the Islamic faith, permits a parent to punish a child in any manner the parent deems acceptable. There is no reason to believe, that is, that when it comes to disciplining a child, "anything goes" in Syria. And if such a line between permissible and impermissible punishment of a child exists in Syria, no indication is given regarding whether Assad remained on the proper side.

The California Appellate Court was right, then, to hold that Assad's requested jury instruction would count as an impermissible comment on the evidence, for the actual testimony at trial hardly supported Assad's claim that his conduct was permissible within his own culture. And Assad would receive no support from a cultural defense if it turned out that his abusive treatment of his son was not sanctioned by the norms of Syrian culture or the Islamic faith. The availability of such a defense is one thing; its success as a defense against a finding of criminal responsibility is quite another. As with *Kargar*, success requires compelling evidence that the defendant's actions do in fact qualify as adherence to the norms of his cultural community; no mere assertion of this fact from friends and relatives will do. And as is invariably the case in a criminal proceeding, the prosecution has every right to question and challenge the accuracy and sufficiency of the evidence in the process of attempting to meet the reasonable doubt standard.

This point introduces an obvious gray area that will haunt the application of the type of cultural defense recommended here. This is illustrated by the slippery slope problem that runs from *Kargar*, through *Moua*, and to *Assad*. As we have acknowledged on several occasions, cultural norms are not uniformly and uncontroversially endorsed and enforced throughout an actual norm circle—something that is rather apparent in *Moua*. Additionally, the meaning and reach of norms that are generally endorsed and enforced throughout an actual norm circle may remain ambiguous and underdetermined. Cultures, once again, are messy things.

When we turn to Category 3 cases, we shall have occasion to say more about the problems this field of gray raises when the concerns of culture are introduced within the context of traditional criminal defense strategies. At the moment, it is necessary only to emphasize that these are problems that can be addressed adequately only within the context of specific cases. They are problems for criminal procedure, in our view, because American criminal jurisprudence should allow for the type of cultural defense supported here. They are, that is, problems associated with the operation and application of the cultural defense, and not problems that produce reason to reject the introduction of a cultural defense into American criminal law.

The cultural defense and inter-cultural affairs

We turn now to our Category 2 cases, which involve inter-cultural conflicts. Cases of this sort introduce controversies in which the government is required by standards of social justice to make sure that all cultural communities tolerate each other in spite of any inter-group hatred, animosity, or misunderstanding that might produce or incline toward conduct that violates a legitimate criminal statute. While some cultural communities might think that their traditional practices and norms permit them to impose themselves upon outsiders, the right of cultural autonomy prevents them from doing so. Consequently, they are not permitted to act upon beliefs or convictions that would allow or even require them to interfere with the opportunity of outsiders to live and believe as they wish. Therefore, the cultural defense is not available to defendants who violate the criminal law as a consequence of actions that also demonstrate the failure to respect the right of cultural autonomy enjoyed by all cultural communities.

Butler: Inter-cultural violence

Some of the more typical examples of this sort of situation are on display in the two cases that comprise Category 2. Consider, for example, *State v. Butler* (1985), which involved three Native Americans who belonged to the Siletz tribe of Oregon. The three defendants were accused of murdering Donald Pier, who had apparently been robbing tribal graves and according to tribal belief disturbing tribal spirits in the process. There was testimony introduced at trial that would indicate the killing of Pier was justified according to tribal belief, and this provides the possibility of imagining the application of a cultural defense in this case.

Once again, the case was decided by a misidentification defense; the State could not establish conclusively that the defendants were Pier's killers. But the case also invites the further consideration of the claim that respect for tribal law and custom should permit the conclusion that Pier's killing was justified if done by tribal members and for the purpose of restoring the peace and tranquility of tribal ancestors. Let us suppose, then, that the defendants did in fact kill Pier and that they elected to defend themselves against a charge of murder by invoking a cultural defense. If we interpret the actions of the defendants generously, we can say that they were implementing tribal justice, and we might even suppose that they were doing so with the blessings of tribal authorities. This does not seem to be the case, to be sure; instead, the defendants acted on their own without the sanction or support of tribal leaders. It may also be the case that Siletz tribal law has formal mechanisms for dealing with offenses against the tribe of the type committed by Pier, mechanisms that were in fact circumvented by the defendants. But we shall presume for the sake of argument that the defendants were merely following tribal custom when they killed Pier, who, we should emphasize, was not a member of the Siletz tribe. This presumption is intended to place the actions of the defendants in the most favorable light from the standpoint of cultural autonomy by suggesting that their actions qualified as legitimate tribal practice.

Let us stipulate, then, that Pier broke tribal law and that the defendants were in some sense authorized by tribal custom to come to the aid of their ancestors and punish Pier for his violation of tribal law (cf. Chiu, 2006, p. 1364). Of course, Pier did more than break tribal law; he also violated several state laws by trespassing upon tribal grounds and robbing tribal graves. So, was Pier answerable to tribal law, to state law, or to both? In Pier's defense, we should note that he had no obligation to obey the laws of the Siletz tribe because he was not a member of the tribe, though he may have had an obligation to obey the laws of the Siletz tribe while on Siletz tribal land. But he did have a legal obligation to respect the property of the tribe under state law. His actions also displayed the greater injustice of failing to respect tribal autonomy by interfering with Siletz burial rituals and robbing tribal graves. This is the sort of thing that the government is required to police and prevent under its justice function, for Pier's disregard for tribal autonomy falls within the broad parameters of the problem of pluralism.

It is perhaps not fanciful to suppose that in his last moments on earth Donald Pier understood and appreciated this last point. His lawless behavior begat further lawless behavior that cost him his life. This is the type of tit-for-tat inter-group conflict that the state needs to prevent in order to manage the problem of pluralism. So, while Pier wronged the Native Americans, he also—and more importantly, as it happens—wronged the entire public. His actions are indicative of the type of behavior that can destabilize the general commitment to social justice that enables disparate groups, cultural communities, religions, and peoples more generally to live together amicably. It follows that Pier should have been prosecuted by the state and that the Butlers and Van Pelt should have let him alone. By living in a civil union where inter-group issues are addressed by state law, the defendants in *Butler* must be presumed to understand that state law trumps any and all tribal authority (let alone individual vigilantism) to police inter-group conflicts to which the tribe is a party.

Therefore, any claim that their culture, heritage, or the like justified the defendants' actions must fall on deaf ears. By virtue of its inter-group character, this is a public matter and not a tribal matter. The appeal to culture or heritage in the process of presenting a defense in *Butler* thus seems sadly out of place. We might understand and appreciate the anger that motivated the defendants, but this is hardly an excusing or mitigating factor. Their actions display a failure to understand the central principle of justice in multicultural settings, namely, that intergroup disputes are to be settled by the neutral authority of the state and that the state has a primary obligation to see to it that all groups under its jurisdiction are tolerated by group outsiders. The right of cultural autonomy, then, does not reach unilateral action against cultural rivals or enemies, and consequently, the cultural defense supported by this right is not available to those who undertake such unilateral action.

Insofar as members of the Siletz tribe held that cultural considerations should protect the defendants in *Butler* from criminal prosecution, they can be presumed to suppose that tribal law and practice were more important to them, or more binding upon them, than deferring to the legal system of the state. But it is just here that the law's claim to authority matters, for to live under a government of law is to live within a political system in which legal machinery exists to settle intergroup or inter-cultural disputes and resolve controversies according to authoritative and acknowledged standards of social justice. The Butlers may have considered themselves more Siletz than American, and they may have resented (no doubt with considerable justification) the historic treatment of their people by the dominant white culture. But this does not override the fact that they now live within a complex multicultural state that needs to live according to authoritative norms that promote a stable and peaceful social atmosphere where all cultural communities can coexist.

Le: Inter-cultural threats

US v. Le (2009), our second Category 2 case, illustrates a similar, albeit more subtle, type of problem. Recall that Le, apparently outraged because his wife was denied a visa to enter the US, mailed a letter to Congressman Scott that seemed, when viewed through the eyes of the majority culture, to issue a significant threat against the Consular Chief in Vietnam, whom Le considered responsible for the denial of the visa. In his defense, Le argued that the contents of his letter, including the reference to decapitation, the smeared blood, and the reference to the 2007 shooting at Virginia Tech, should be understood in the terms of his own native Vietnamese culture, and when understood in these terms, their meaning is really quite benign and non-threatening. Le's claim, in effect, is that cultural information about his method of expressing himself would indicate that he was innocent of the charge of mailing a threatening communication.

If Le is correct that his method of communication in his letter to Congressman Scott was intended to insult and not to threaten, and that it would be so understood by members of the Vietnamese community, then there would be no legal issue had Le sent his letter to a member of his own cultural community. But he did not do this, and presumably he well understood that Congressman Scott was not a member of the Vietnamese community. His lack of familiarity with English, and perhaps his failure to integrate even modestly into mainstream American society, may provide some explanation for his actions, but it is another matter to suppose that this explanation should qualify as a defense for otherwise criminal conduct. Conduct that is appropriate within the context of one's own cultural community may not be considered appropriate outside one's cultural community, and it seems worth emphasizing that all members of a multicultural society should have some appreciation of this point. Le's misstep, in effect, was his failure to recognize this point, and this amounts to a failure to appreciate that when one steps outside the borders of one's own cultural community, one will be held responsible for following the norms that regulate and direct inter-cultural activities and communications. This too is a form of respecting the autonomy of different cultural communities.

Le's criminal offense, needless to say, is not as morally significant as the offense committed by the defendants in *Butler*. And perhaps it is not unreasonable to suppose that the charges against him should have been dismissed or at least mitigated on the grounds that he simply did not know any better. But we do not need an independent cultural defense to reach this conclusion. Le's lack of appreciation of the fact that his cultural ways might be misunderstood when they were pursued outside his culture can hardly be supported or demonstrated by any appeal to the right of cultural autonomy. All that is required to clarify Le's actions is to explain the meaning his communicative techniques carry within his native culture. But an appreciation for Le's inter-cultural naïveté should not blind anyone to the fact that he remains responsible for understanding and respecting the political obligations that ride with citizenship in a multicultural community.

The public standards of conduct that operate inter-culturally are necessary in order to facilitate the operation of social life in a multicultural state and diffuse the problem of pluralism. The *Le* case is illustrative of the kinds of controversies that will invariably arise when these public standards are not grasped. It bears repeating that the endorsement and enforcement of those valued political norms that bind the US into a common polity is crucial for peaceful coexistence in a multicultural context.

The members of minority cultures who wish to retain their native language, religion, beliefs, and cultural ways are entitled to do so according to the right of cultural autonomy. But this right has a flip-side; it generates a duty that requires the members of all cultural communities to respect the ways of all others. This means, among other things, that shared standards of politeness are necessary to manage and regulate inter-cultural dealings, communications, and associations. Immigrants cannot be required to abandon their cultural ways and practices upon entering a new country, but they can be required to learn how to get along amicably with their new neighbors. So, while sympathy for Le's inter-cultural myopia might be understandable, it hardly seems sufficient to forgive him for his decided lack of inter-cultural manners.

Cultural autonomy and the cultural defense

The discussion in this chapter has been rather winding and complex; therefore, a few remarks by way of argument summary are in order. A survey of the way certain cultural questions have been introduced into the American criminal justice system has indicated that sometimes these questions trigger a concern for the right of cultural autonomy. When this happens, we argued that a cultural defense is in order to protect defendants who are merely engaging in their own cultural practices and/or following their own cultural norms against criminal prosecution.

It was also argued that the availability of a cultural defense ends when allegedly criminal conduct exhibits an inter-cultural aspect. A defendant cannot invoke a right to cultural autonomy for actions that violate her or his own obligation to respect the members of different cultural communities. There are still other situations where the claim of cultural autonomy will not support a cultural defense against criminal prosecution. These arise when a defendant engages in some practice, or follows certain norms, that are no longer endorsed and enforced by her or his cultural community or that are generally not considered endorsable and enforceable norms by the general population of the culture or by cultural elites. The challenges and difficulties these cases raise for criminal procedure will be engaged briefly in the final chapter.

Notes

1 We differ, in this regard, from Wanderer and Connors (1999. pp. 868–872), who conclude that *Kargar* demonstrates that cultural factors can be assimilated within existing constitutional and statutory law (e.g., by the effective application of things like *de minimis* statutes) without additional need for a distinct cultural defense.

2 We put rape in quotation marks to indicate that this terminology does not accurately represent the Hmong practice, for the Hmong concept of rape is rather different in meaning from the definition in American criminal law. A brief account of the Hmong notion of rape, or what seems to qualify as the Hmong notion of rape, follows shortly.

5 Culture and the Constitution

The discussion of the previous chapter suggests that the right to cultural autonomy can be invoked as a legitimate criminal defense in the event state prosecution involves an intrusion into the cultural affairs or activities of some minority cultural community. It remains to be seen, however, how such a defense might be built into the architecture of American law and how it would function in criminal jurisprudence. The purpose of this chapter is to argue that if the right to cultural autonomy can be defended as a fundamental constitutional liberty, then the cultural defense that follows from it would involve the assertion of a constitutionally protected right.

Identifying the right to cultural autonomy as a fundamental American liberty that supports a cultural defense also introduces the possibility of a more uncompromising approach to the problem of pluralism than is currently available in American law because of judicial reliance upon the great American compromise. We will also develop and defend this possibility below. Acknowledging a cultural defense intended to protect minority cultural practices, the argument goes, should replace the great American compromise as the proper way to resolve disputes that arise when dominant majorities attempt to impose their own ways and beliefs upon vulnerable minorities. While this point of view will no doubt seem unduly radical and offensive to many, it would merely put an end to an enduring contradiction, and an embarrassing double standard, in American law and politics by honoring the traditional American ideals of equality and liberty. By making toleration a living reality in American law, it would also move the country closer to its professed commitment to, and belief in, the ideal of justice for all.

Immunity rights

In his classic discussion of the notion of "a right" in law, Wesley Newcomb Hohfeld noticed that sometimes the concept of right identifies or expresses a legal immunity. Hohfeld understood an immunity to involve "one's freedom from the legal power or 'control' of another as regards some legal relation" (Hohfeld, 1919, p. 60). Accordingly, an immunity can be considered a type of exemption; to have an immunity right is to be exempt from the legal control of some agent with regard to some sphere of action (Hohfeld, 1919, p. 62). To put the point in more directly Hohfeldian language, if A has an immunity right with regard to X (something over which A has control), then there is some B (person, group, state, etc.) that is disabled from interfering with A's control of X. The right to cultural autonomy, as we have developed the notion here, can be considered an immunity or exemption in this sense. By virtue of this right, cultural communities are exempt from outside interference in their internal affairs.

Because this right is derived from the fundamental political norms of the land, we can think of it as a political right. Accordingly, the defense of this right throughout the body politic should be a basic responsibility of government in general and the judiciary in particular. This is most evidently accomplished, in the field of personal interactions, by means of the criminal law. Unwanted and objectionable intrusions into the affairs and lives of some group of people by some other group of people almost invariably involve some violation of the criminal law. This is, in large measure, a result of the fact that such transgressions violate some criminal statute protective of individuals, separately as well as collectively. While these statutes are not specifically or perhaps intentionally designed to protect a right to cultural autonomy, they effectively do so by protecting the individuals whose cultural autonomy is imposed upon by individual citizens acting either independently or in concert. Here the normalcy and justice functions of the law just happen to dovetail.

To illustrate, the State of Oregon has criminal statutes that prohibit theft and trespass. Presumably, these laws are intended by the state to protect all persons from acts of theft and trespass undertaken by all other persons. Like similar statutes in other criminal jurisdictions of the US, they are culturally driven—they operate as defenses of certain culturally embedded norms involving the transference of goods and the protection of personal property (the normalcy function), but they are also culturally blind. They look through or past culture and recognize only certain personal interactions held to be objectionable according to the norm system of the majority culture. It does not follow, however, that they cannot be put to use by the state as mechanisms for the protection of the right to cultural autonomy (the justice function). Thus Oregon theft and trespass statutes presumably protected the burial grounds of the Siletz, even if the State of Oregon had no specific criminal statute on its books that protected the Siletz tribe or its traditional burial grounds from trespass or plunder by outsiders. If we suppose the tribe owned the tribal artifacts stolen by Donald Pier, as well as the land in which the artifacts were buried, then Pier had no right to take them, and had a correlate duty not to take them.

If the right to prevent others from taking tribal artifacts protects the Siletz from Donald Pier and others, however, it is not because the right in question should be understood legally as an instance of the right to cultural autonomy. If the Oregon legislature had acted specifically to protect the Siletz against outside aggression or intrusion of any sort, including the protection of tribal burial grounds, then we might infer that Oregon intended to provide protection for tribal autonomy. But if protection of tribal burial grounds was left to general theft and trespass statutes, then the tribe enjoyed the legal protection that all persons in the State of Oregon enjoy against theft and trespass at the time Pier plundered their tribal burial grounds.

Yet while the ordinary standards of criminal law afford groups and cultural communities some degree of protection against outside interference, they are not necessarily fully protective of cultural autonomy, or as fully protective as the right to cultural autonomy would seem to require. National civil rights legislation designed to address similar or related problems in the area of racial justice might be modified to provide some degree of support for the right to cultural autonomy. But even with the addition of federal civil rights requirements, the legal protection for cultural autonomy would remain rather meager.

Further protection of cultural autonomy might be found in the use of legal exemptions to state and federal legal obligations. Criminal statutes can, and on occasion do, threaten the autonomy of religious and cultural communities. This occurs, for example, if and when criminal law prohibits certain conduct considered permissible, or perhaps even essential, according to the norm system of some religious or cultural community. In cases where the criminalization of some conduct is considered appropriate or even morally necessary according to the norm system of the majority culture, but where the norm system of some minority culture allows or even promotes the conduct in question, states have often had recourse to legal exemptions. The use of such exemptions is controversial and not without critics (cf. Barry, 2001, pp. 87–88). But in general the use of the exemption strategy seems a sensible and effective way to permit the majority culture to prohibit conduct held to be objectionable according to its norm system and still protect the opportunity of minority or satellite cultures to live as they wish regardless of whether some of their practices are objectionable to the majority communities around them.

The great problem with the exemption strategy, however, is that it depends upon the sympathies of legislatures, with regard both to whether an exemption is granted and to its nature and reach. Kent Greenawalt has noted that exemptions may be either specific or general, with the difference resting upon the comprehensiveness of the exemption granted (Greenawalt, 2014, p. 172). Presumably, specific exemptions might target particular groups (e.g., Catholics during prohibition) and exempt them from specific legal requirements (e.g., the use of alcohol). But such exemptions might be more general in either of two ways: first by extending exemptions to group identifiers (e.g., religious communities, cultural communities), and second, by extending exemptions to general legal requirements (e.g., religious practices that might transgress any number of specific legal requirements). General exemptions, in turn, would involve both these more general features; they would apply to group identifiers and reach or cover general group practices.

Given the great diversity of cultural communities in the US, along with the variety of practices and diversity of beliefs collectively present within them, the use of specific exemptions, while perhaps both useful and appropriate in certain circumstances, is not likely to secure a viable right to cultural autonomy for all minority cultural communities. And no doubt relying upon this strategy would overburden legislatures and make a mess of state (and federal) statutes. The use of general exemptions, however, might prove to be a profitable legal strategy for immunizing the right to cultural autonomy against intrusion and abuse by the majority culture. As Greenawalt rightly observes, "Any need for a general cultural defense depends partly on the legislature not having achieved all the desirable accommodations to cultural practices through specific exemptions" (2014, p. 155).

But it is not clear whether a general exemption strategy alone could meet the challenge of fully supporting the right to cultural autonomy for all minority and satellite cultures. In practice, legal exemptions, at both the state and federal level, tend to be sprinkled around like a kind of legislative grace. Minority cultures may request such exemptions, but they cannot demand them. And it is unlikely that the granting of such general exemptions to particular minorities will receive much legislative support in the event the groups in question are held in disfavor for whatever reason by the dominant majority.

One way to mitigate, but not defeat, this problem is suggested by the wording of the ill-fated Religious Freedom Restoration Act (RFRA) that was passed by Congress in the wake of the Supreme Court decision in *Employment Division v. Smith* (1990). This Act was designed to restore the Supreme Court's compelling state interest test, abandoned by the Court in *Smith*, in order to provide more protection for the free exercise of religion.[1] This test, as noted previously, holds that the free exercise of religion immunizes religious practitioners from criminal prosecution unless the state has a compelling interest in preventing practitioners from engaging in certain of their religious practices and provided the resultant intrusion into these religious affairs is the least drastic measure for achieving this interest.

The success of a similar general exemption extended to minority cultural communities would depend in large measure on what would qualify as a compelling state interest. Greenawalt thinks that "this language will not help people who commit intentional homicides or inflict serious physical harm; the government has a compelling interest in preventing that behavior" (Greenawalt, 2014, p. 174). But fashioning a coherent account of an interest sufficiently compelling to warrant state intrusion into the internal workings of some cultural community may not be as straightforward as Greenawalt apparently thinks. There is trouble lurking, for example, with his presumption that the state has a compelling interest in preventing "serious physical harm." The test, reminiscent of Mill's harm principle, takes us back to the great American compromise; it allows the majority culture to decide what counts as a compelling interest by interpreting the notion of "serious physical harm" in terms of its own normative perspective (cf. Nussbaum, 2008, pp. 179–199).

This problem seems practically unavoidable because the notion of harm drips with cultural significance, both in terms of what counts as harm and in terms of when and why it is reasonable or appropriate to risk such harm. It might make sense to a member of the majority culture for a person to risk this harm if it is the possible (even likely) outcome of a surgery needed to save this person's life, but not if doing so was necessary to the process by which, say, a young man moves in his culture from childhood to manhood (cf. Greenawalt, 2014, p. 162). This construction of the compelling interest test, in short, repeats the great American compromise because the presumption behind it is that the understanding of harm that produces a compelling state interest is the understanding at home in the majority culture. (If the minority culture's sense of harm was employed here, the compelling interest standard would never be reached.) This means that only minority practices considered inoffensive according to the standards of the majority culture would enjoy protection under a RFRA-inspired exemption while such practices considered offensive and intolerable by the majority culture would not. This does not seem like much support for the right to cultural autonomy.

These comments are not intended to suggest that an exemption strategy is not a welcome legislative approach to the defense of the right to cultural autonomy. No doubt some degree of support for this right can be managed through the use of exemptions, but it seems unlikely that a sufficient legal defense of the right to cultural autonomy can be realized by reliance upon the exemption strategy alone. Before we could expect much legislative support for the kind of general exemption required to defend the right to cultural autonomy, we would need to see considerable political support for this right. This, in turn, is possible only if an appreciation for the demands of social justice, and an awareness of the consequent need to practice toleration with regard to cultural variety, is cultivated throughout the body politic. But ironically, if such political enlightenment should ever come about, it would bring with it a natural commitment to tolerate cultural difference, and in this event, the legal defense of the right of cultural autonomy would hardly be necessary. The right matters politically, and hence legally, only where there is political sentiment that supports its abridgement.

Cultural autonomy and civil liberty

The above comments indicate that existing legal support for the right of cultural autonomy is not altogether meager. But it is hardly as robust as it might, and arguably should, be. While existing criminal statutes in most, if not all, states, in conjunction with federal civil rights legislation, seem sufficient to protect the members of cultural minorities from the private impositions of ordinary citizens, this degree of protection falls rather short of the general immunity from state intrusion into the internal affairs of minority cultural communities promised by the right of cultural autonomy. This general absence of protection for cultural autonomy is most notable in the *Crow Dog* decision discussed above, but it is also evident, though to a lesser degree, in both *Kargar* and *Moua*.

Had a cultural defense been available in these cases, Crow Dog would not have had to face a finding of criminal responsibility for the same act from two distinct legal jurisdictions, and Kargar would not have needed to take his case all the way to the Supreme Court of Maine in order to realize what seems on its face to be a fairly obvious and appropriate outcome. Similarly, Moua would not have been placed in a situation that pressured him to accept criminal responsibility for something he most likely did not do because the California criminal justice system had to struggle through an in-house dispute between hostile Hmong families and clans that seems comprehensible only in terms of Hmong culture and internal Hmong politics.

This is reason to think that the introduction of a cultural defense in American law would offer significant and meaningful additional support for the right of cultural autonomy. Consequently, it is now worth considering how a cultural defense might actually work, within the architecture of American criminal jurisprudence, as a criminal defense. We have suggested that a cultural defense would defend against a finding of criminal responsibility by immunizing defendants against criminal prosecution. This shifts the general understanding of the defense away from questions about whether it should operate as a justification or as an excuse—the exclusive focus of the narrow, legalistic approach to the subject mentioned at the outset of the discussion. Both justification and excuse concede the state's jurisdiction over some criminal prosecution and attempt to defeat a finding of criminal responsibility by noting extenuating circumstances regarding a defendant's actions or mental state (Chiu, 2006, pp. 1326–1332; Renteln, 1993). On our account, a cultural defense would enable a defendant to establish that her or his conduct, whether offensive or not in the eyes of the majority culture, is immune from legal prosecution.

Defenses of this sort are hardly unheard of in American law, though they are not usually thought to belong to the realm of criminal jurisprudence. They issue, instead, from some formative legal document—a constitution, in effect—that contains an account of the limitations upon the reach of governmental power/authority. Such limitations are typically understood in American constitutional law to be civil liberties, or spheres of personal/group freedoms (liberties) into which government (state, federal, or both) cannot legally intrude. Civil liberties, in short, are immunity rights that exempt their holders from the reach of governmental power/authority. Since the right to cultural autonomy qualifies as an immunity right, there is good reason to think that a cultural defense might be understood as a way of invoking the right of cultural autonomy in order to immunize minority defendants against federal or state criminal prosecution.

This nod toward constitutional law in support of a cultural defense is hardly original. Kargar apparently wanted to press such a claim. Renteln claims that Kargar argued on appeal that his conviction for violating the Maine gross sexual assault statute violated "his constitutional rights to due process, freedom of religion, parental autonomy, and privacy," all rights guaranteed him under the federal Constitution (Renteln, 2004, p. 245 n. 53; Greenawalt, 2014, p. 172). This might seem like a motley list of rights that only talks around Kargar's genuine constitutional concern, but if we think of this concern in terms of a right to cultural autonomy, it should be readily apparent that no such right is officially listed in the document. Yet this is not an end to the matter, for if the federal Constitution is a document designed to breathe life into the American spirit of social justice, it should be possible to interpret the document in a fashion that can support the right of cultural autonomy.

But is it possible to make a compelling argument for the view that the federal Constitution provides civil liberty protection to minority and satellite cultures that would limit the authority of government to intrude into their internal affairs? This question can be understood to ask whether it is possible to locate within the US Constitution a right of cultural autonomy that would immunize minority defendants against criminal prosecution under certain specified circumstances (our Category 1 cases), thus establishing a constitutional foundation for a cultural defense. We propose now to examine three possible strategies of argument for extending civil liberty protection to cultural minorities. We do so mindful of the limitations of Madison's "parchment barriers against the encroaching spirit of power" (Madison, 1961, p. 308). Although civil liberties are designed to protect minorities against majorities in democratic societies, the best defense of social justice in any state is surely an enlightened citizenry. But failing this, it often falls to the judiciary to remind the citizenry of its commitment to social justice (the justice function of law), and the best way to engage the judiciary in this challenge is to provide vulnerable minorities with the legal weaponry necessary for their defense in the event their internal practices make them targets of criminal prosecution.

The free exercise of religion and cultural autonomy

The first constitutional strategy for defending a right of cultural autonomy to be considered makes appeal to the religious liberty clauses of the First Amendment. We noted previously that intergroup conflict in colonial America generally took the form of religious conflict. Thus the subject of concern that initially shaped and influenced the concern for liberty across the land involved religion, and this historical artifact is on display in the special protection that religion receives under the First Amendment. This opens up two possible avenues of argument in support of a First Amendment foundation for the right of cultural autonomy. First, we might notice that culture and religion seem to overlap (Greenawalt, 2014, pp. 172–73; Waldron, 2002, pp. 24); or in the terms that follow from our account of culture, that religion is a part of culture.

Cultures, as that notion is used here, are norm circles (communities) identifiable by virtue of their commitment to certain politically salient norms that are endorsed and enforced amongst their members, *and* they are identifiable by virtue of the fact that they stand in antagonism to one another by virtue of the normative difference associated with these politically salient norms. Some of the politically salient norms that may define a particular norm circle (cultural community) may be understood or conceptualized, by members of the circle *or* by outsiders, as religious norms. Moreover, nothing of importance hangs on the question whether a specific norm qualifies as religious, moral, ideological, or (more comprehensively) cultural. What matters is that the politically salient norm is endorsed and enforced, as a salient norm, by some norm circle, which is a way of saying that it matters to those who endorse and enforce it.

The religious clauses of the First Amendment, reflecting early American history, single out a set of group norms, identifiable within the cultural milieu of a Christian religious inheritance, for special protection. The reason for this is that these particular norms are politically salient; they happen to matter greatly to those communities whose members hold them, and they contradict certain politically salient norms held by different communities—communities that qualify as different by virtue of their normative disagreement (Waldron, 2002, p. 24). (Think yet again of Roger Williams and John Cotton.) Waldron, following Michael Dorf, has suggested that such norms have a special claim on those who hold them because they have a "*social* reality" (2002, p. 24, emphasis in original). But not all cultural norms that matter greatly to those who happen to hold them need be conceptualized as religious norms. If these also have a social reality, as they surely do, it would seem that they are deserving of a similar protection. It is, after all, the salience of the norm that matters, and not the historic characterization that the dominant cultural community elects to give to it. This would extend First Amendment protection to minority cultures and allow their members to hold the norms that matter to them, and engage in the practices they value without fear of criminal prosecution driven by the fact that others disapprove of what their members believe or what they want to do.

The second avenue of argument for a First Amendment defense of cultural autonomy requires a somewhat different answer to the question why religious norms should be singled out for constitutional protection. This response suggests that religious norms receive constitutional protection not because of their religious nature, but because of their historically divisive nature. Religious conflict was worrisome in colonial America because it was a source of *political* unrest, uncertainty, and instability. As we argued previously, the first step toward an appreciation of freedom, and thus toward a concern with social justice, involved recognizing the need to identify political principles that could establish social peace and stability by putting an end to intergroup conflict and/or oppression. The religious clauses of the First Amendment effectively do this by taking religious matters off the political agenda and leaving religious communities free to practice their faiths as they see fit.

Freedom, on this view, is valued as a necessary condition of political stability and social peace, and the key to this freedom is the toleration of difference. So, the spirit behind the religious clauses requires a general commitment to the toleration of difference; this is the freedom that these clauses safeguard, with the religious attachment providing testimony only to the source of the conflict that produced an appreciation for the value of freedom. Read in this historical and philosophical context, then, the free exercise of religion can be understood to protect difference, and since this is precisely what the right of cultural autonomy requires, it is possible to find in the defense of religious liberty the defense of a more capacious cultural liberty as well.

Cultural autonomy and freedom of association

A second possible constitutional strategy for defending the right of cultural autonomy involves arguing that this right is implied by the judicially created right of free association. In the 1958 decision of *NAACP v. Alabama*, the Supreme Court held it to be "beyond debate that freedom to engage in association for the advancement of beliefs and ideas is an inseparable aspect of the 'liberty' assured by the due process clause of the Fourteenth Amendment" (1958, p. 460). This, of course, is precisely what cultural communities do as a matter of course, and consequently, it follows that they should be accorded associational rights protection.

Associational rights are often regarded as predominantly political rights; they safeguard groups whose members come together in the pursuit of legitimate political objectives. But association for the purpose of pursuing things that matter to the members of the group formed by their association need not be limited to political affairs in the narrow sense of pursuing some specific political or policy agenda. In a larger sense, all groups whose members seek to practice their own ways and pursue ends that matter to them are political units seeking the liberty to live as they wish. So, if it makes sense to insist that there is a right of free association implied by the due process clause of the Fourteenth Amendment, it would seem to comprehend the right of cultural communities to live as they wish, for this is the point and purpose of their association.

Due process of law and cultural autonomy

The third possible strategy for defending a constitutional right of cultural autonomy is suggested by the second. Rather than rely upon the derivative right of free association, we might simply get straight to the point by holding that a right to cultural autonomy is implied by the due process clauses of the Fifth and Fourteenth Amendments. This is where we would like to focus our attention, because it provides the most inviolable grounding for the protection of cultural autonomy. If we can, in fact, recognize group autonomy as an implied fundamental right through substantive due process, then the cultural practices of a group will be beyond the reach of interference by government.

Though this strategy depends upon the questionable notion of substantive due process, the judicial practice identified by this notion is now a familiar feature of American constitutional law. Consequently, we are inclined to think that there is no longer anything horribly objectionable about insisting that certain basic rights are built into the constitutional mandate that federal and state governments cannot abridge liberty "without due process of law." If one is willing to concede a claim of substantive due process—and the Supreme Court has certainly done so for other fundamental rights now recognized as such—then this strategy of argument gets to the heart of the matter rather quickly.

Yet, appealing to substantive due process does necessitate holding that the emergence and/or evolution of fundamental political principles in constitutional law is often a historically contingent and culturally specific affair. The historical contingency behind the development of these principles is illustrated by the fact that they frequently, if not typically, emerge as a consequence of political efforts to establish social peace and secure political stability. These notable ends are realized by resolving the destabilizing social conflicts in need of political remedy by means of the political articulation of controlling political norms that all parties to the conflict can accept and endorse. This, as should be apparent, is the process by which a political culture emerges and political units move away from domination and toward social justice.

The cultural specificity of these principles is displayed by the fact that their practical legal articulation is typically driven by the nature of the social conflicts they are designed to resolve. As noticed previously, for example, the ideal of freedom in the US was initially articulated, at least in constitutional terms, by the introduction into the document of a series of "great rights" that would carve out spheres of liberty (e.g., religion and speech) that political elites believed essential to check the power of the central government. This articulation has expanded, in ways that do not always employ the notion of freedom, as the political culture has developed to accommodate various groups, racial, gender, and now ethnic, in a way that permits them access to the rights and opportunities historically and traditionally enjoyed by the more dominant elements of the body politic.

Valued freedoms, in short, come to be valued as a consequence of political and social struggle. The political cultures of non-authoritarian states are shaped as a result of this struggle, and the shape this culture takes is contingent upon the types of basic principles introduced to resolve or mollify the struggle in need of political remedy. But this is not a process that ends at some magic moment. The constant and continuing re-creation of difference guarantees that the political culture of non-authoritarian states is invariably a work in progress into the future. The process of the historical re-articulation of the ideals of the political culture continues and expands as new struggles emerge. As a result, the basic principles employed to end conflict and secure political legitimacy receive an increasingly general and comprehensive restructuring through time. Put somewhat differently, the formulation of these principles is expanded as their spirit is generalized in order to address effectively whatever new social conflicts happen to emerge.

The general re-articulation of fundamental political ideals is aided in non-authoritarian states by reliance upon the rule of law and a politically neutral judiciary that can approach this process in a principled and non-partisan fashion. But re-articulation is not invention, and therefore, if the judiciary is to do its job, it must be able to point to some formative tradition or document that initially identifies, albeit in terribly imprecise ways, the ideals in need of re-articulation. In the US, of course, and at least at the federal level (though increasingly at the state level as well), the formative document is the federal Constitution.

Because the ideal of freedom encompasses the right to cultural autonomy—because the latter is really a dimension of the former, respect for this right should control both political and legal approaches to the challenges produced by the problem of pluralism in the US. This simply bows in the direction of the traditional and enduring American commitment to the ideal of freedom for all. The immediate problem before us, however, is to locate a legal foundation for this right in the federal Constitution. And perhaps the most viable way to do this is to regard the right to cultural autonomy as an analytic feature of the liberty safeguarded by the due process clauses of the Fifth and Fourteenth Amendments. We shall consider both clauses together because there is reason to think that the conception of liberty at home in the Fourteenth Amendment is consistent with, if not identical to, the conception present in the Fifth Amendment.

The US Supreme Court has recently issued an opinion that echoes several of the sentiments expressed in the above paragraphs. The Court's decision in *Obergefell v. Hodges* (2015) addressed the controversial question of the constitutionality of same sex marriage. The Court concluded that this marriage qualifies as a fundamental right that holds against states under the due process and equal protection clauses of the Fourteenth Amendment. In the process, the Court noted that the ideal of freedom/liberty is invariably a work in progress because it is impossible to grasp "the extent of freedom in all its dimensions" through abstract reflection alone (2015, p. 2598).[2] Therefore, "the generations that wrote and ratified the Bill of Rights and the Fourteenth Amendment . . . entrusted to future generations a charter protecting the right of all persons to enjoy liberty as we learn its meaning" (2015, p. 2598). This meaning is learned, we have suggested, as ideals crafted from the vicissitudes of historical conflict receive re-articulation as more generalized principles that are then employed to resolve new political and legal controversies.

There must be some normative anchor to the process, of course, and the anchor the Court adopts in *Obergefell* is the "dignity and autonomy of persons." This decidedly liberal ideal is what fundamental rights are presumed to protect in the eyes of the *Obergefell* majority. And we might suppose, in good liberal fashion, that freedom matters because it is the condition *sine qua non* of showing respect for the "dignity and autonomy of persons." But if we suppose that persons are essentially and inescapably cultural beings, it is but a small step from acknowledging respect for the "dignity and autonomy of persons" to acknowledging a right of cultural autonomy.

Let us stay for the moment with the Court's reasoning in *Obergefell.* The case involved a claim by the gay and lesbian community to a fundamental constitutional right to marry that was legally unavailable to members of this community in several states. The Court found Fourteenth Amendment due process protection for this right on the ground that persons should not be denied the important right to marry by virtue of sexual orientation. As should be apparent, the gay and lesbian community endorses a set of sexual norms, and thus engages in certain sexual practices, that are neither endorsed nor enforced by the heterosexual majority that surrounds them. Thus on matters of sexual orientation, the gay and lesbian community also has standing as a distinctive cultural community. (If it sounds odd to suppose that the gay and lesbian community has its own culture, it is worth noting that this follows from the way the notion of culture is being employed here. What matters in this regard is the political salience of the norm(s) that separates actual norm circles and places them in political conflict; for present purposes, the comprehensiveness of the norm clusters held by these norm circles is irrelevant to the fact of cultural conflict because this conflict typically orbits around specific norms.)

The states in litigation had in place legal barriers that prohibited gay and lesbian participation in the practice of marriage. These barriers were in place because the politically dominant view in these states was that marriage was a sacred bond between a man and a woman, a view that was rejected by the gay and lesbian community.[3] This issue does not trigger concerns about the right of cultural autonomy, of course, because this right would reach only the opportunity of cultural communities to practice their own ways as they wish, and the homosexual community was asking for the right to participate in a legal practice operated and managed by the state. But the homosexual community did indicate, by virtue of the litigation, that at least some of their members wished to participate in the practice of marriage because marriage was of normative importance to them. Therefore, they were denied the right to engage in a practice that mattered to them by virtue of certain normative convictions that are opposed, often aggressively, by elements of the more dominant heterosexual community.

It is important to be clear on precisely what the Court believed the due process and equal protection clauses of the Fourteenth Amendment protected in *Obergefell*. If the fundamental right deserving Fourteenth Amendment protection was the right to marry, then the case would protect participation in a practice treasured by the majority culture for cultural communities holding norms (and thus engaging in practices) considered anathema by the majority culture. This reading takes us some distance away from the right of cultural autonomy. But the gap can be closed if we suppose that the Court wanted to extend due process and equal protection to cover the right of a minority cultural community to engage in practices that matter to them regardless of the opposition the majority culture has to the norm system of the minority community in question. On this reading, the fact that the gay and lesbian community claimed the right to engage in a socio-legal practice endorsed by the majority culture is only incidental. What matters is the right of the gay and lesbian community to engage in a socio-legal practice that its members endorse and in which they wish to participate.

In other words, it is the right of some cultural community to follow the norms and engage in the practices that matter to its members, and not just the right to engage in the practice of marriage, that should properly receive Fourteenth Amendment protection on this reading. This becomes clearer if we reverse the reasoning and notice that the *Obergefell* decision holds that the majority culture cannot deprive minority culture A of the opportunity to do X (a practice the majority culture happens to endorse) because the minority culture practices Y (a practice the majority culture happens to disdain). It is acting upon the disdain for Y by, in effect, discriminating against A, that raises a concern for the dignity and autonomy of the As here, and not merely the fact that the discrimination in question prevents the As from participating in a practice that matters to the dominant culture and the As alike.

On this reading of *Obergefell*, the argument of the majority would strongly support a Fourteenth Amendment due process and equal protection case for the right to cultural autonomy. The respect for the dignity and autonomy of persons, that the Court considered in *Obergefell* to drive the process by which we learn (develop) the meaning of freedom, should be understood to support the idea that persons (cultural beings) have the right to live by the norms they endorse and enforce amongst themselves and to engage in the practices that they consequently hold dear. What else could it mean to display respect for the dignity and autonomy of persons (cultural beings), and what else could it mean to value freedom as a fundamental right?

A cultural defense apology

Each of the above constitutional arguments provides a strong case for the constitutional recognition of a right to cultural autonomy. Though we consider the substantive due process argument the most compelling of the three, there is much to be said for all three. If one or more of these arguments is sufficient to put to rest concerns about the constitutional acknowledgement of a right to cultural autonomy, the case for a cultural defense follows as a matter of course. Such a defense would simply involve the legal showing that the criminal prosecution of some individual intruded upon that person's right to cultural autonomy. Examples of the prohibited intrusions are on display in our Category 1 above. This includes the *Assad* case, though it seems likely in this case that the appeal to such a defense would fail unless Assad could provide greater evidence to the effect that his actions fell within an acknowledged Syrian and/or Islamic practice for disciplining children.

But before we can turn to our Category 3 cases, there is a bit more to be said in support of a cultural defense in American criminal law. The idea of a cultural defense is not without its critics, and the reasonable concerns they raise deserve a hearing. Sometimes these critics produce specific objections to the use of such a defense, and sometimes they merely express some genuine worries about its place in criminal jurisprudence and its prospects for abuse (cf. Renteln, 2004, pp. 192–194). In general, both sorts of objections and worries are directed at an understanding of the cultural defense that puts it in the camp of legal excuse or perhaps legal justification, rather than the camp of civil liberty protection against governmental intrusion. Nonetheless, several of the objections present in the literature may be applied to our construction of the defense, and therefore, we shall close this chapter with a careful scrutiny of four objections we consider the most challenging.

The objections we shall consider go as follows. 1) The absolutist objection: a civil liberty defense of the right to cultural autonomy seems to hold absolutely against state authority, but this is too strong a claim—civil liberties should not be considered absolute. 2) The arbitrariness objection: deference to culture arbitrarily exempts the members of minority cultures from an obligation to obey the law because there is no reason to value culture over other variables that might explain illegal conduct. 3) The equal protection objection: deference to culture in criminal law creates dual, or multiple, legal systems that variously protect disparate cultural communities in opposition to the ideal of one system of law for all. And 4) the intolerable practice objection: civil liberty protection for cultural minorities would block the ability of the state to intervene in objectionable cultural practices that harm more vulnerable members of these communities, thus leaving the more vulnerable without important legal protection. We shall consider each objection in turn.

The absolutist objection

The case for a right to cultural autonomy is too strong, or objectionably strong, because it seems to afford absolute civil liberty protection to religions and minority cultures. The idea that civil liberties are not absolute is considered by many to be a staple of American constitutional law. But the above argument intimates that there are no limits to the right to cultural autonomy, and this is unacceptable.

This objection is easily defeated, however, by noticing that nothing in the above argument insists that a right to cultural autonomy holds absolutely. While it is true that the argument is intended to block (and to block uncompromisingly) state interference in the practices of minority cultures, it does not follow that the recommended civil liberty protection is absolute. In fact, the argument may fall into line with the traditional judicial sentiment behind the recognition of limitations upon constitutional guarantees, a sentiment that has not always been respected by the judiciary itself.

The US Supreme Court has traditionally and properly held that civil liberty protection of fundamental rights is not absolute. As we have seen, for example, prior to *Employment Division v. Smith* (1990), the Court employed the compelling state interest test, discussed previously, to decide when the free exercise of religion had to yield to a state interest. While this approach did not produce the great American compromise (the *Sherbert* test (1963) came into prominence well after *Reynolds* (1879)), it did nothing to eliminate it either. The test would support the *Reynolds* decision, for example, if one holds that the state has a compelling interest in prohibiting the practice of polygamy. But the problem with this legal approach to monitoring the reach of fundamental rights is that there is no clear standard for determining what is to count as a compelling state interest. Disgust or repugnance on the part of the majority culture, for example, may be premised upon the presumption that some practice harms its participants in some way, and this could be used as grounds for finding a compelling interest in preventing the practice in question. This is the problem that haunts the great American compromise, even though it looks as if this is the very thing that civil liberty protection is intended to defend against.

However, it is possible to clarify what should count as a compelling state interest if we draw a distinction between the justice function of law, on one hand, and the general responsibilities and obligations of citizenship on the other. The foundation for this argument was established above and involves the distinction between primary cultures (the actual norm circles that fix an individual's basic norm cluster) and the political culture (the norm circle fixed by citizens who endorse and enforce the fundamental norms of civil association that define the meaning of social justice in practice). People (all of whom are identifiable as members of some discernible cultural community or some discernible set of such communities) should enjoy the right to live according to the norm or norm clusters of the cultural communities (norm circles) to which they belong (the right to cultural autonomy), but as members of the cultural community (norm circle) that is the state, they also have an obligation to adhere to the obligations of citizenship incumbent upon them by virtue of their membership in this cultural community.

People *qua* citizens have an obligation to meet the requirements of citizenship and to do their fair share in the process by which civil association is sustained and managed. In the event a rule of civil association conflicts with a group norm, all citizens (whether they belong to minority or majority norm circles) are obligated to obey the rule of civil association, even if this requires them to amend or abandon certain practices associated with their primary cultures. Thus the Wisconsin Amish could properly be permitted to remove their children from public schools after the eighth grade, for this removal—required as a defense of the Amish norm circle according to the Wisconsin Amish (*Wisconsin v. Yoder*, 1972)—did not render Amish children incompetent citizens or otherwise compromise their ability to meet their civil obligations. Things were clearly different, however, when the Amish asked to be excused from paying social security taxes (cf. *United States v. Lee*, 1982). The national social security system requires general citizen involvement if it is to be successful, and consequently, the establishment of a national retirement fund produces a general obligation upon all citizens to participate in the system.

Cultural communities with deep normative objections to legitimate obligations of citizenship may, of course, request an exemption from them, but they have no right to claim immunity from these obligations by virtue of their religious convictions or cultural beliefs, for the obligations of citizenship must be held to stand upon a compelling state interest. Insofar as such exemptions are granted, they do resemble a kind of political grace, for they are granted as a result of legislative deference rather than legal right. The granting of conscientious objection status is perhaps the classic example of an exemption of this sort. The demands of national defense impose an obligation of citizenship on all citizens (and particularly in a state boasting a republican spirit), and this obligation is sufficiently compelling to override First Amendment free exercise challenges. If, however, the federal Congress wishes to permit such exemptions, it is certainly entitled to do so.

Because the obligations of citizenship trump civil liberty protections (e.g., legitimate national security issues trump free speech guarantees), we can think of them as compelling when they come into conflict with some civil liberty guarantee, and therefore, civil liberties cannot be considered absolute. This construction of the compelling interest test specifies rather explicitly what is to count as a compelling state interest, namely, a genuine obligation of citizenship—those obligations necessary for the preservation of the state, the promotion of national welfare, and the advancement of social justice. None of these concerns is endangered if the native Americans in *Smith* (1990) are allowed to receive unemployment benefits by virtue of the fact that the practice of their religion involves the use of Peyote or, for that matter, if the Mormon community is allowed to practice multiple marriages. There are reasons why a collection of peoples (religions, cultures, races, and so forth) might come together for the purpose of civil association, and these reasons power and underlie the consequent obligations of citizenship these peoples assume as a result of their participation in the state, but the desire to impose one's religious, moral, or ideological views on others who subscribe to different norms is not (and ought not be) one of them.

The arbitrariness objection

This objection is not too far removed from the absolutist objection. The claim that cultural autonomy is entitled to protection as a fundamental right works as a legal defense in the event a defendant establishes that she or he violated an otherwise valid criminal statute or regulatory ordinance as a part of a legitimate cultural practice. This effectively immunizes minority cultural communities not just from state efforts to endorse and enforce important norms (in the form of criminal statutes) accepted by the majority culture (the normalcy function of law), but also from morally less significant general regulatory requirements. It does so by identifying one particular feature of persons (viz., cultural identity) for the purpose of defeating findings of criminal responsibility. It may be objected, however, that focusing upon this particular attribute of persons is rather arbitrary and serves to privilege this feature of persons over others (e.g., poverty, poor parental oversight, etc.) when it comes to judgments of criminal responsibility (cf. Lacey, 2014, p. 52). But why should culture be considered special in this way?

We noted earlier that Jeremy Waldron has answered this question by claiming that religious and cultural practices have what he calls a "*social* reality" (Waldron, 2002, p. 24, emphasis in original). This social reality is present for persons in the form of a "scheme of regulation" that places one under a "burden grounded in the actually-existing and well-established regulation and coordination of social affairs afforded by a religious or a cultural tradition" (Waldron, 2002, p. 24). Waldron is responding to an argument pressed by Brian Barry that challenges religious exemptions (and by extension cultural exemptions) from regulatory laws on grounds of arbitrariness (Barry, 2001, pp. 40–50). Waldron's argument is that religious and cultural norms regulate personal behavior in a particularly strong and binding manner, and this distinguishes them from other, more idiosyncratic reasons for doing/not doing some putatively illegal action that do not belong to religion or culture.

Religions and cultures really do this of course, but does this mean that they deserve legal immunity, or exemptions, from criminal and regulatory statutes? (For present purposes we shall suppose no difference of importance hangs on the distinction between an immunity (right) and an exemption (legislative grant).) Waldron's argument reduces to the uninteresting claim that religions and cultures should be exempted from valid regulatory laws because they are religions and cultures—norm circles in which certain identifying norms considered to be politically salient are endorsed and enforced. This is certainly true, but Barry's argument pushes deeper than this, for what he wants to know is why religions and cultures are sufficiently special to deserve exemptions from valid regulatory statutes (Barry, 2001, p. 48). And we cannot reply to this by insisting that the something special is that they are religions and cultures, or (what amounts to the same thing) that they are norm systems that occupy a place of importance in the value schemes of those holding them. It is always meaningful to ask why religions and cultures deserve exemptions or are owed immunities, and it is not very helpful to answer this by repeating that they are religions and cultures.

A more compelling response to Barry can be presented if we appreciate the way in which legal immunities, or immunity rights, and exemptions are lodged within the political culture of the state itself. This involves repeating the central leitmotif of our argument: religious difference, once an extraordinary source of political conflict and social unrest, was accommodated by recourse to the (political) practice of toleration in order to secure social peace and domestic tranquility. If the incentive for embracing religious toleration was prudential, the norm produced by this prudential decision requires the toleration of those normative differences that shape the borders of different peoples. In other words, the political culture of historically liberal states establishes the grounds upon which immunities and exemptions are premised and justified. Immunities of this sort are a strategy for the accommodation of difference, and the history of liberal states reveals the evolution of a political commitment to tolerate difference by devising and implementing such accommodationist strategies.

Therefore, singling out cultural communities for immunity from criminal and regulatory statutes is hardly arbitrary at all. While these communities are not intrinsically special, they have come to occupy a special place in the norm system of our political culture. And this special place is identifiable in terms of the right to cultural autonomy (or religious liberty, and so forth) that drives the legal immunities and exemptions we now believe these communities deserve. Other differences that are excluded from consideration for legal immunities or exemptions fail to qualify for such things because they have different histories. Consequently, individuals separated by these differences still fall under the normalcy function of law because the differences on display do not represent a politically salient distinction between them.

The equal protection objection

According to this objection, a right to cultural autonomy is inconsistent with the equal protection of the law because it effectively creates dual or multiple legal systems that differentially protect those subject to them. This objection need not detain us long. It comprehends a litany of fairly modest concerns that are easily addressed. First among these is the familiar concern that incorporating a cultural defense into American criminal law would create separate standards of justice for different people, a concern that we have addressed in our earlier discussion of social justice. We have only one standard of justice, but it respects various normative differences by immunizing those who hold different normative postures from being imposed upon by majority views and beliefs. The right to cultural autonomy simply adds another dimension to the religious and racial protections already present in American law.

This might seem to dismiss what may appear to be a strong objection to the cultural defense rather quickly. In its most dramatic form, this objection involves the fear that "the absence of a uniform legal code will lead to anarchy" (Renteln, 2004, p. 192; cf. Choi, 1990). But the recognition of a cultural defense as a feature of the right to cultural autonomy can hardly be presumed to endanger "a uniform legal code;" instead, it actually belongs to such a code and helps to establish its uniformity. It helps establish and defend the autonomy and integrity of different cultural minorities within society and protect them from abuse by majorities whose members claim the moral right to use the coercive might of the state to impose their will on others. Because this is a central dimension of the American commitment to freedom, any risk that the use of civil liberties to protect minorities against majorities might produce anarchy would seem to be worth running. Ironically, such civil liberty protections actually guard against the threat of anarchy by mitigating the intergroup conflict that would result in the absence of religious and cultural toleration.

It could also be argued, of course, that a cultural defense is subject to possible abuse; groups and individuals might invoke this defense as a strategy to escape legal punishment for violating laws they do not like or might find profitable to disobey. This claim reduces the objection to a practical problem, however, that is already with us and has already been addressed in the context of First Amendment free exercise jurisprudence. The objection supposes that the courts will be unable to distinguish between genuine claims of cultural autonomy and deceitful attempts to use the cover of culture as a way to escape legal punishment by groups or individuals whose legal transgressions are not the consequence of adherence to recognized cultural norms. While it may prove difficult to draw a perfect line between these situations, such a technical difficulty is hardly reason to abandon a commitment to honor the cultural autonomy of minority cultures. If drawing an exact line between deserving cultural communities and criminal subterfuge is difficult, the attempt must still be made, just as it must be made in the area of religious freedom.

The equally familiar "When in Rome" argument also belongs to this family of objections. This argument contends that immigrants have an obligation to assimilate into the dominant culture, form a common people, and embrace the (legal) norms that indicate how things are done here. To live in America, one might say, one must be or become an American—that is, endorse and enforce the norms of the dominant culture, and of course this takes us back to the normalcy function of law. It is tempting to dismiss this argument outright because in its most familiar form it is both silly and unrealistic. Its silliness stems from the fact that the United States is already a terribly pluralist society, along with the accompanying fact that cultures tend to fragment even without the introduction of outside influences. And it is unrealistic because one can hardly expect culturally diverse immigrants to slough off their culture at the border, shift normative gears, and transform themselves into "average" Americans.

The temptation to dismiss this objection quickly should be avoided, however, because there is something of importance to it. We have noticed this already when we discussed our Category 2 cases: all cultural communities must endorse and enforce the norm system constitutive of American political culture. So the insistence that immigrant cultural communities have an obligation to assimilate into the dominant culture is, in fact, on target, and in this sense we can say that immigrant cultural communities do have an obligation of citizenship to become American. The meaning this notion carries, however, needs to be understood in distinctively political terms, for being an American is a distinctively political condition (cf. Walzer, 1996; Shklar, 1997). In saying this, we are aware that the flames of nativism and xenophobia still burn bright within the land; we are aware that the notion of being an American remains contested and controversial across the political landscape. But if the political norms signaled by concepts such as freedom, equality, and justice are to have any place and importance in American political life, they must be understood to signal an appreciation of and respect for difference—*real* difference and not just a tepid difference of taste.

So, this understanding of the equal protection objection is right to suppose that immigrant groups need to assimilate into political life in America, but it is wrong to suppose this means that immigrant groups must integrate into the ways of the dominant culture. Because the right to cultural autonomy is a compelling norm within the norm system of American political culture, it should be recognized and respected by all Americans. This is what is right about the "When in Rome" argument. The argument goes wrong, however, when it confuses the norm system of American political culture with the various norm circles that produce majority or dominant views on normative matters, and the confusion—or conflation of the political with the social—is itself a threat to those American political ideals that support the right to practice different ways, worship different gods, and value different things.

There is one final version of the equal protection objection that needs consideration. According to this version, disadvantaged or victimized groups within certain cultural communities may be denied the equal protection of the law if the cultural defense protects their abusers from criminal prosecution (Coleman, 1996). Because the victims of abuse within cultural communities deserve legal protection, and because a cultural defense might undermine such protection, the defense should not be allowed, or at least not allowed in cases where some (typically men) victimize others (typically women and children). To allow the defense in these cases would leave the women and children of abusive minority cultures more vulnerable to abuse (Goldstein, 1994, p. 161).

The concerns raised by this objection push beyond equal protection issues, however, and are shaped in terms of equal protection only because this makes a good legal approach to the real problem at hand. And the real problem is that some cultural practices are considered to be so morally objectionable by some thinkers that they are simply beyond the parameters of the tolerable. To illustrate, consider again the Hmong practice of "marriage by capture." If the practice really does involve kidnap and rape, or if this is just a male strategy for taking a bride by kidnapping and raping a woman, then its abusive character should be apparent enough, and if law is a means for preventing one person from abusing and harming another, then it should be employed at this point to protect women from being subjected to such treatment (Coleman, 1996, pp. 1127–1128). So, the concerns raised by this objection take us to the fourth and final objection to the cultural defense that we shall consider.

The intolerable practice objection

It is hard to say if this is the most powerful objection to the introduction of a cultural defense in American criminal law, but it is certainly the most popular. Its appeal rests with the fact that it enlists powerful moral sympathies at home in the communities whose norm systems are dominant within the body politic. And at this point in the discussion it should also be rather familiar, for it is a variation of Mill's harm principle employed to justify blocking cultural practices considered harmful to some in the eyes of those who appeal to the argument. The problems associated with getting clear on the nature of harm built into the objection have already been introduced. But it is time to provide a more studied review of this objection in order to thoroughly evaluate its merits. We shall begin with some preliminary remarks that should help clarify the basic problem that troubles this objection.

To start, we want to repeat a central fact about social life: the social environment is in constant flux (cf. Giddens, 1979, pp. 198ff.). Discussions of culture are made problematic, not simply because the concept is rough around the edges, but also because the norms or norm clusters that identify cultures are always changing—shifting and drifting on the historical tides. Cultural drift is particularly problematic in pluralist states because intersectionality produces cultural cross-fertilization that brings, or can bring, even the most firmly entrenched group norms into question. The result is intra-cultural conflict. This conflict is also fueled by inter-cultural criticism and controversy, as external political influences incline elements of some cultural community to reconsider previously held norms. Thus inter-cultural conflict can also drive intra-cultural conflict.

The legal system in pluralist states is likely to become involved in these many-faceted culture wars. Law, and in particular the criminal law, can be regarded as an instrument of conflict—a weapon of war, so to speak—both within and between cultures. Aspects of this social phenomenon have already been mentioned. The normalcy function of law, for example, works as a conservative force in society insofar as it figures in the process through which the majority culture endorses and enforces its defining norm system. And we have also seen that the advocacy function of law can contribute to the prospects for social conflict. Law serves the end of social change when members of some powerful or dominant cultural community enlist the help of the legal system to promote their policy objectives (cf. Lernestedt, p. 2014).

Minority groups are easily caught within the grips of these culture wars. Sometimes this is because minority cultural practices are offensive when measured by norms held in great regard by the majority or dominant culture. At other times minority group practices become the targets of criticism because they resemble or exemplify the workings of norms that are considered deeply objectionable by certain social elements pressing for basic normative change throughout society. The first of these challenges to cultural autonomy is evident in the US by virtue of the moral revulsion the majority culture directs at such practices as Islamic honor killings, female genital mutilation, and the Hmong practice of "marriage by capture." The second of these challenges is evident in the concerns expressed by many feminist theorists that the multicultural movement in the United States may support the abuse of women and children within minority communities by shielding abusive practices from public scrutiny and censure. As Susan Okin put it, "Establishing group rights to enable minority cultures to preserve themselves may not be in the best interest of the girls and women of those cultures, even if it benefits the men" (1999, p. 23).

In general, this objection challenges the view that minority groups should be accorded a right to cultural autonomy that completely immunizes them from interference by majority groups. But it is also employed on occasion to raise specific concerns about the introduction of a cultural defense in American criminal law. Alice Gallin, for example, has insisted that "cultural defenses should not be used because the United States should not allow other cultures, which do not respect individual liberty and equality in the same manner as American culture does, to subvert the value we place on preventing domestic abuse" (1994, p. 725). One can understand and appreciate Gallin's nervousness; such practices as honor killings and marriage by capture most certainly do "shock the conscience" of the vast majority of Americans. And it is probably little solace to note that these things shock the modern conscience in much the way Roger Williams's separatism shocked the conscience of his Puritan brethren, who would also not allow him to "subvert the value" they placed on devotion to God.

But it is hardly clear why Gallin thinks the American respect for liberty and equality is on her side, or why this respect necessitates the prevention of domestic abuse as abuse is understood by those political forces who wish to oppose it. As the more theoretical chapters of our discussion illustrate, the liberty to which Gallin refers matters within American political culture because it protects difference, and it protects this difference whether we like all instances of it or not. So, Azizah al-Hibri's reply to Okin can be directed toward Gallin as well: "If western feminists are now vying for control of the lives of immigrant women by justifying coercive state action, then these women have not learned the lessons of history, be it colonialism, imperialism, or even fascism" (al-Hibri, 1999, p. 45). The lesson involves noticing the danger to freedom in a political atmosphere where people think "the best community" is one in which all but their preferred practices are outlawed (al-Hibri, 1999, p. 45).

While these comments may not defeat the intolerable practice objection, they do appear to leave us with something of an impasse—a normative conflict of sorts. On one side of the equation stands the fundamental norm of social justice: the ideal of freedom requires tolerating difference. On the other side of the equation stands something like the basic *grundnorm* of liberal morality: respect the dignity and integrity of persons by honoring them as autonomous agents. If this impasse is inspired, at least in part, by the fact of inter-cultural conflict, it is also primarily a matter of intra-cultural tension and disagreement. It is, this is to say, a problem within American liberal political culture which espouses a commitment to justice and a concern for the basic well-being of persons. And the question—a central, if not *the* central question behind the enterprise of political philosophy—posed by this impasse is this: which norm trumps the other?

The all-or-nothing sound of this question may be objectionable to those who think it possible to find some satisfactory compromise to this conundrum. This appears to be the strategy employed by Alison Dundes Renteln, one of the most dogged and eloquent defenders of a cultural defense in American law, who is willing to "ask ethnic minorities to surrender their traditions" in the event the practice of these traditions results in "irreparable harm" to some members of the community (Renteln, 2004, pp. 15, 217; Greenawalt, 2014, p. 174). Renteln is aware of the challenges associated with recourse to such a nebulous notion as harm (2004, p. 217), but this does not deter her from stipulating that certain imagined physical events cause the sort of irreparable harm she finds morally objectionable. Since it seems silly to suppose that Renteln merely invented her list of irreparable harms, it is highly likely that the list reflects her own cultural biases; the damage or hurt done to persons by these practices seems, according to her norm system, to qualify as harm, and she would permit the state to coercively interfere with such practices in order to protect those involved.

But Renteln's argument, and similar others (e.g., Greenawalt's, discussed above), offers no real solution to the impasse between the norm of social justice and the norm of liberal morality; instead, it leads back toward the great American compromise. Majority groups here are willing to tolerate minority practices as long as they do not run afoul of group norms that incline their members to regard them as so immoral as to qualify as intolerable. Nor can this problem be overcome by invoking the rhetoric of rights at this point and arguing that the right to cultural autonomy is overridden when some minority group engages in a practice that violates (some majority group's sense of) human rights. Seen from inside a moral point of view, this may make a good deal of sense; but seen from a more neutral (if not objective) vantage point, it merely asserts that the moral norm from which liberal rights are derived trumps the norm of social justice. And this takes us back to square one.

If compromise is not possible (because it defaults in favor of the norm of liberal morality), it is necessary to choose. And if we must choose, it is altogether likely that liberal spirits will opt for the norm of liberal morality. But we should remember here that we are being asked to choose between two norms that will serve as the foundation of the political morality of a pluralist state. And remembering this may incline us to recall, and appreciate anew, al-Hibri's response to Okin, for our choice should reflect and honor the "lessons of history." The chief lesson of history that matters here—learned from, among other things, the religious travail of the seventeenth century—is that the moral self-certainty that inclines some to impose their will upon others, no matter how well-meaning, poorly serves the ends of social peace and civil tranquility. This is why the norm of social justice was initially, if only obscurely, embraced within a nascent United States.

It might be worthwhile at this point to refer one final time to the case of Roger Williams, for the argument used to produce the Bay's decision to banish Williams was simply a very early version of the intolerable practice objection. Williams's soul freedom would merely turn Satan loose to work his will against those unable to discern religious truth, and this would do great—in fact, extraordinary—harm to the flock of the faithful. So, anyone attracted to the intolerable practice argument will need either to accept the outcome of Williams's trial or find some strategy to distinguish Williams's situation from their favored use of the objection. If this strategy involves challenging the Puritan understanding of harm brought against Williams, they will then need to explain their own confidence that their account of harm is objectively valid. Similarly, those who would opt for the justice function of law in Williams's case, would seem by parity of reason to need to do so in all similar cases where the intolerable practice objection is employed to question the goal of justice.

So it seems that when viewed against the background of this historical perspective, the choice of principles becomes rather obvious. The reason we have a norm of social justice is to trump the kinds of imperious actions likely to be pursued by cultural majorities because they find the practices of others morally intolerable. Its pride of place is the lesson of history that al-Hibri recalls to mind. In a state that claims to be a beacon of freedom, this is the choice that must be made (al-Hibri, 1999, p. 45). It is a choice that acknowledges the priority of political wisdom over moral certainty. If one would make this into a moral lesson, it would then follow as a matter of course that the tension between the norm of social justice and the *grundnorm* of liberal morality dissolves. To allow others the freedom to live as they wish and practice their cultural ways, as we emphasized in our discussion of *Obergefell*, simply is to respect them by honoring their dignity and autonomy. Conversely, to respect others and honor their dignity as autonomous beings would also require cultural outsiders to allow them the freedom to live as they wish and practice their cultural ways, free from the coercive interference of the state.

Conflict and cultural change

The above conclusions obviously recommend rejection of the intolerable practice objection, but there is still more that needs to be said on this score. While the right to cultural autonomy is not absolute, it is uncompromising; it prevents one lot of people from coercively interfering in the affairs of another lot of people no matter how repugnant the ways of that lot of people might seem to others. This way of putting the matter is intended to help avoid problems associated with the inclination to reify the notion of culture. Because we have elected to understand culture in terms of politically contested norms and norm clusters (Elder-Vass, 2010; 2012), cultural communities are recognizable in terms of, and separated by means of, their distinctive and politically salient normative commitments. Accordingly, the right to cultural autonomy protects norm circles whose members endorse and enforce (one or more) norms that place them in conflict with norm circles whose members endorse and enforce different and opposed normative convictions.

This is the view that underlies our primary response to the intolerable practice objection. Let us consider again feminist concerns that the right to cultural autonomy would protect cultural communities they consider abusive toward women and children (Okin, 1999; Nussbaum, 1999). And we might add to the discussion ancillary concerns that the right to cultural autonomy would leave minority groups within minority cultures powerless against the more dominant social forces in their communities (cf. Eisenberg & Spinner-Halev, 2005). Because the right to cultural autonomy protects groups from the unwanted coercive (and only coercive) interference by outsiders, whether this interference is taken by government officials or private individuals, it disempowers outsiders from inserting themselves into internal group affairs and politics to address these concerns.

It follows that feminists can continue to complain about cultural communities they consider sexist and abusive, but they must still tolerate these communities, just as these communities must tolerate them and put up with whatever criticism feminists press against them. But the issue raised by the concern for minorities within minorities requires a bit more discussion. In one sense, that talk of minorities within minorities may be rather misleading, for politically salient normative disagreement separates people into distinctive communities no matter what they might otherwise share in common. In another sense, however, talk of minorities within minorities is altogether appropriate. Groups have their own internal politics, and the way the resultant political struggle might play out introduces reason to make an important qualification to our response to the intolerable practice objection.

The fluid nature of group life makes the job of defending the right to group autonomy tricky business. The particular difficulty to which we wish to call attention at this point is produced by the fact of social change and cultural evolution. What happens when normative disagreement creeps into otherwise generally homogeneous cultural communities and begins to divide the population? Consider again the "marriage by abduction" practice of the Hmong. It is possible this practice has changed with the Hmong presence in America, perhaps making young Hmong men more inclined to kidnap Hmong women in order to secure a bride (Evans-Pritchard & Renteln, 1994, p. 15). And it is also possible that Hmong women have begun to gravitate toward norms controlling the treatment of women at home in the majority culture around them; it is possible, that is, that intersectionality is working normative change amongst the Hmong population, change that is particularly embraced by Hmong women.

Such change politicizes the "marriage by abduction" practice. If Hmong women begin to insist that they will no longer tolerate this practice, thus splitting the Hmong community into distinct gendered cultures holding conflicting marital norms, it would become incumbent upon Hmong men to tolerate Hmong women on this score, and the failure to do so is no longer an intra-cultural matter. It becomes, instead, a failure to respect the cultural autonomy of Hmong women, and the cultural defense would not then reach a Hmong male who argued against prosecution for kidnap and rape on the grounds that he was engaging in this practice. This illustrates the process of group mitosis; two norm circles now exist because disagreement on the "marriage by abduction" practice has become politically salient and now separates Hmong men from Hmong women. Had it been clear that this was the situation involved in the *Moua* case, then the case would fall into Category 2, and a cultural defense would not have been available to Kong Moua.

A similar point can be pressed with regard to the Islamic honor killing issue. In the event that Muslim women elect to oppose this practice by virtue of the fact that they now endorse and enforce different social or religious norms, it becomes the business of the state to use the criminal law to defend this norm circle against the unwanted coercion of the male members of Islamic families who would impose their own sexual norms on these women.[4] In all probability, determining when group mitosis has taken place, or when normative disagreement remains an internal cultural matter, will not be easy. The right to cultural autonomy means that the criminal law cannot put culture on trial. It would prohibit state prosecutors from hauling the members of minority cultures into court for engaging in practices governed by norms that are endorsed and enforced within this community. But this right presumes that all the practitioners involved really do endorse and enforce, grudgingly or otherwise, the norms that govern these practices.

If there is evident political opposition to such norms by some lot of people, who break with their parent culture on this score, or if an individual is imposed upon by others in spite of her or his expressed opposition to the practice or activity at hand, there is strong reason to suppose that group mitosis has taken place and there are really two distinct cultural communities present here, identifiable by the political salience that surrounds the different norm(s) endorsed and enforced by the two groups. Such discriminations are not easily made, but this is no reason to abandon the right to cultural autonomy or a culture defense in criminal law. These are practical matters that must be judged, and this, of course, is a proper provenance of the criminal trial process. While theoretical reflection can indicate how the line should be drawn, the actual drawing of the line must be left to the specific facts and circumstances of actual cases. But theoretical reflection can help judges identify the crucial questions that need to be asked in circumstances of this sort.

Strong defenders of the intolerable practice objection will not likely find great solace in these remarks, but they have not been offered in order to deflect any apparent power this objection might be presumed to have. It remains the case that this objection involves what we consider a misplaced moral reaction against the political commitment to toleration, and thus against the lessons of history as well. But it is important to recognize that the right to cultural autonomy does not end normative conflict and the social change it drives. Instead, it operates within a shifting and agonistic cultural milieu, and this makes the legal and political challenges associated with endorsing and enforcing this political norm difficult and complex. On the one hand, the state is prohibited by the right to cultural autonomy from intruding itself into the internal affairs of minority cultural communities, but on the other hand, the state is required to defend the autonomy of cultural communities (norm circles) from coercive interference by outsiders. The boundaries at issue are fixed by the political salience of normative disagreement that separates communities, and thus the matter to be judged involves an analysis of the depth and principled character of the normative differences at issue. The proper reach and application of the cultural defense lies within these murky parameters.

Notes

1 The Supreme Court later overturned RFRA as it applied to local and state jurisdictions. See *City of Boerne v. Flores* (1997).

2 We say "freedom/liberty" here in order to signal that we are treating these concepts as synonymous, though we are mindful of some modest difference in their respective meanings. See Pitkin (1988).

3 The politically dominant view need not be the majority view, of course, for a minority might be able to marshal the political resources necessary for the realization of their own interests in opposition to the majority. While this might seem rare in democratic political systems, it is hardly unheard of. In general, however, the politically dominant view will dominate because it constitutes the majority norm circle with regard to some normative conflict.

4 This argument does not provide solace for those who worry that children would still be "victims" of abusive cultural norms because children lack the political standing in the community to affect normative change. But of course the power of intersectionality can work on parents as well, and perhaps exposure to the child-rearing norms of the majority culture will encourage some degree of change. If this can be hoped for by those who worry about the abuse of children, the matter remains subject to the evolutionary flow of cultures themselves. This, too, is a consequence of respecting the right to cultural autonomy.

6 Culture and criminal responsibility

This completes our discussion of the need for a cultural defense in American criminal jurisprudence. But there remains for consideration the troubling and eclectic cases that fall within our Category 3. These cases do not raise concerns about respect for cultural autonomy because the activities of the defendants do not qualify as acceptable or acknowledged cultural practices. But both cultural norms and practices have been alleged to be pertinent to considerations of criminal liability in these cases, and thus it is worth asking whether cultural variables might factor into the process by which criminal liability should be measured in these and similar cases. That is the purpose of this chapter.

To refine the subject of inquiry somewhat, we propose to ask here whether the right to cultural autonomy might also entail an obligation of cultural deference in cases where cultural variables are germane to questions of criminal responsibility but a cultural defense, of the sort defended above, does not apply. While we will ultimately reject the possibility of such an entailment, we will also provide reason to think some legal inquiry into cultural factors is valuable for a precise appraisal of a defendant's criminal liability. The guiding principle behind our analysis is that persons ought not be punished if they have done nothing wrong. But the understanding of the wrongfulness of one's actions can vary across cultural communities, and it is this fact that counsels in favor of considering cultural matters in the process of criminal litigation. This is tricky business and it is easy for participants in the criminal justice system to misuse cultural data with the unfortunate result of misdirecting the aims of criminal justice.

Cultural variation and criminal law

There is probably no entirely satisfactory method for resolving the various cases belonging to Category 3. But they often find their way into the criminal justice system, and therefore, it is necessary to say something about them, if only to appreciate the challenges and tragedies they often involve. Both challenge and tragedy swirl around the first case that falls into this category: *People v. Kimura* (1985).

To recall the facts of the case, Fumiko Kimura drowned her two children as part of her decision to follow the ancestral Japanese custom of *oya-ko-shinju*, or parent-child suicide. Kimura's actions followed an extended effort to find some resolution for her husband's infidelity, and the failure to do so led her eventually and perhaps desperately to attempt *oya-ko-shinju*. Though she succeeded in drowning her two children, bystanders pulled her from the water before she was able to end her own life. She then faced criminal prosecution for the death of her children.

The defense argued that Kimura's decision to pursue this practice was an indication of her temporary insanity, a position supported by testimony from six psychiatrists (Woo, 1989, p. 406; Renteln, 1993, p. 463; Chiu, 2006, p. 1350). The claim was that Kimura's decision to practice *oya-ko-shinju* demonstrated her insanity; Kimura, at the time she drowned her children, lacked the cognitive control to distinguish right from wrong (Kim, 2006, p. 205; Kim, 1997, p. 119; Chiu, 2006, p. 1350). The judge eventually accepted a plea bargain that reduced the charge to voluntary manslaughter, and Kimura was sentenced to a year in jail (a sentence she had already completed) and five years' probation (Renteln, 1993, p. 463).

As it stands, the case illustrates the way cultural information may be used to help gauge the mental state of a defendant at the time a crime is committed, and thus to help measure the extent of wrongfulness, if any, displayed by the criminal act. Insofar as such information is necessary for these assessments, it seems altogether appropriate to allow it as evidence in a criminal proceeding. This hardly qualifies as cultural defense as this notion is understood, however, because the operation of this defense does not address the wrongfulness of a defendant's actions. The cultural defense defended above establishes that a defendant has done nothing wrong if her allegedly criminal actions belong to some accepted and acknowledged cultural practice. Additionally, an inquiry into a defendant's mental state at the time of her or his allegedly criminal act is a standard feature of criminal defense, and the fact that cultural information may be relevant to this inquiry hardly justifies thinking of this as some sort of cultural defense.

Beyond this, it could be argued, there is nothing else to say; this is about all the case illustrates. Consequently, we should not worry further about it. But this rather easy dismissal of the issues presented by the case may poorly represent the way cultural factors actually figure into, and help shape, the challenges the case presented to the California criminal justice system. This is certainly the view of Elaine Chiu (2006), for example, who thinks that the cultural elements of the case suggest the propriety of a justification defense rather than the (partial) excusing conditions actually employed in Kimura's defense.

Chiu rejects the idea that Kimura suffered from diminished cognitive capacity at the time she drowned her children, and argues instead that Kimura's actions should be considered justified on the grounds that resort to parent-child suicide under the circumstances was the least harmful resolution to her love triangle predicament (Chiu, 2006, p. 1353). A claim of justification based upon a showing of lesser harm is not as outlandish as it might seem in this case, but to appreciate the point, it is necessary to understand the place *oya-ko-shinju* has, or has had, in Japanese culture. Chiu makes her case first by noting that suicide in Japan is acceptable for persons who "suffer from certain insurmountable obstacles" (Chiu, 2006, p. 1352). Assuming Kimura faced such an obstacle, a decision to commit suicide is complicated by the fact that Japanese culture considers it wrong for a mother to abandon her children; therefore, the traditional practice (*oya-ko-shinju*) is for the mother facing such an obstacle to kill her children before taking her own life (Chiu, 2006, p. 1352).

On this account of the circumstances surrounding the case, Fumiko Kimura was hardly insane at the time she drowned her children; instead, this account would have us believe that she was perfectly rational and functioning effectively as a moral agent within the norm system of her own culture. "Fumiko Kimura and the California Penal Code simply differed as to whether her particular act of *oya-ko-shinju* was morally right or wrong" (Chiu, 2006, p. 1351). But this claim is misleading for several reasons. For one thing, Kimura is hardly the final authority regarding when and why it is appropriate for a Japanese mother to practice *oya-ko-shinju*. Cultural practices are rule-governed affairs, and to engage in these activities involves following the appropriate rules. So, the propriety of Kimura's actions are neither entirely nor exclusively her call; her actions must still meet the expectations and evaluations of her cultural community.

As it happens, the practice of *oya-ko-shinju* was no longer an accepted or condoned practice in Japan at the time Kimura killed her children, and it also does not appear that it was accepted or condoned by the Japanese-American community in Los Angeles to which Kimura was attached—arguably making this community her actual norm circle. While Chiu tends to minimize the point, this fact is directly pertinent to the moral critique of Kimura's actions. If the Japanese norm cluster no longer endorses or enforces the norms that underlie parent-child suicide, then it would seem the practice no longer has any normative standing within the Japanese community. If it did have such standing, *Kimura* would readily fall within our Category 1; it would be equivalent to what transpired in *Kargar*.

But because parent-child suicide no longer has such standing, it cannot be a Category 1 case. And it is clearly not a Category 2 case because Kimura did not impose her own cultural ways on outsiders in a manner deemed criminal by the State of California. But as Chiu points out, it seems misconceived to think the case presents us with a garden-variety question of murder because cultural data make it difficult to view Kimura as a garden-variety murderer. Chiu's conclusion, that "Kimura's act of drowning her children was not an act that needed to be excused, but rather an act that needed to be explained" (Chiu, 2006, p. 1354), is not entirely warranted, however.

For one thing, the explanation that Chiu provides does not get Kimura completely off the insanity hook. Kimura did appear to plan her actions, though rather apparently under considerable stress, but reasoned actions that demonstrate the ability to achieve a chosen end are not sufficient to establish sanity; people of questionable sanity are often able to pursue bizarre ends in a strategically rational manner. The question of insanity depends upon Kimura's cognitive impairment throughout the process by which she reached the decision to commit *oya-ko-shinju*;

while she can be presumed to have acted in the manner she deemed proper, the issue is whether she was capable of distinguishing right from wrong at the time she reached this decision. She may, for example, have known that *oya-ko-shinju* is no longer morally condoned within Japanese culture but was so overwhelmed by the stress, embarrassment, and shame that she was unable to appreciate this and fell back instead on old and now discredited cultural norms.

The propriety of an insanity claim used to introduce excusing conditions, then, is actually conditional upon whether it was in fact the case that Kimura suffered from a cognitive defect during the time she made and executed her decision. But the cultural information emphasized by Chiu makes the claim that Kimura did suffer from diminished capacity a hard sell. At the very least, it demonstrates that we should not automatically infer that Kimura was suffering from diminished capacity simply because she killed her children in the process of attempting to end her own life, for the cultural information about *oya-ko-shinju* establishes that this is a practice a reasonable and mentally capable Japanese mother in similar circumstances might decide to follow.

But proceeding upon the presumption that Kimura was a responsible moral agent at the time she killed her children does not make the disposition of her case any easier. Even if we concede this point, it hardly follows that her actions should be considered justified. The lesser harm claim seems doubtful in this case because Japanese culture no longer condones, and in fact condemns, the practice of *oya-ko-shinju*. It could be argued, of course, that Kimura was simply unaware of this, or refused to accept the cultural shift away from parent-child suicide, but neither of these factors necessarily makes Kimura any less culpable. If change is the aim of cultural authorities who criminalize once-traditional practices, ignorance of the change, or the steadfast dedication to now discredited ways, can hardly serve as much of a defense. In this situation, ignorance of the law cannot support the conclusion that Kimura's actions were justified.

So, there is little doubt that Kimura did something wrong according to the norms of her own norm circle. But the problem posed by the case is to decide upon the extent of the wrongfulness reflected by her actions. This, in turn, involves getting clear on the actual crime Kimura committed. If Chiu's cultural explanation is accepted, it would be sufficient to say that Kimura intended to kill her children, and in fact she did so. This is simply a feature of the practice of *oya-ko-shinju*. Therefore, she acted deliberately and purposively to end the lives of her children, and under American criminal law, this looks a lot like first degree murder (Chiu, 2006, p. 1349). If, following Chiu, we rebut this by arguing that Kimura's actions followed traditional Japanese cultural practice, we must face the fact that the norms upon which these actions were based are no longer accredited features of the prevailing Japanese norm system. Thus Kimura would be considered culpable in Japan for what she did, but her wrongdoing, it seems, would not reach the level it would reach in California for a finding of intentional homicide.

This gets to the heart of the reason why the *Kimura* case is so troubling. From a standard American perspective, it looks like Kimura murdered her children. She acted purposively and deliberately to bring about their deaths. But the introduction of information about Japanese norm systems may well incline even a fairly hard-hearted American to entertain a degree of sympathy for Kimura's actions. With this information in place, she does not seem to be the horrible monster her actions would otherwise make her out to be. If we think the punishment must fit the crime, we are in trouble in Kimura's case because American law does not seem to make available a crime that fits the reduced degree of punishment that Kimura apparently deserves. So it is tempting to seek out mitigating factors by packaging the relevant cultural information in a way that suggests diminished capacity. Chiu is perhaps right to expose the apparent fraud on display in this move (assuming that Kimura was not actually suffering from diminished capacity—an issue it seems impossible to resolve under the circumstances), but her recourse to justification is unsatisfactory because the Japanese norm system does not support this conclusion.

Perhaps we can make some headway here by noting that descriptive accounts of conduct do not necessarily provide an adequate understanding of a person's actions because actions themselves are often intelligible only as cultural artifacts (Searle, 1995; Winch, 1958). Voting, for example, may involve making some marks on a piece of paper, but not all instances of making marks on a piece of paper qualify as voting. The social meaning of action was also noticed in Kargar's actions as discussed above. To bystanders in Maine, it seems that Kargar's action of kissing his son's penis displayed sexual abuse, but to an Afghan the actions displayed fatherly love. This illustrates the way that the meaningfulness of Kargar's action is lodged within his cultural community and certain practices indigenous to this community. And the same would seem to be true of Kimura's actions when she killed her children. She was engaged in the practice of *oya-ko-shinju*. If the meaning of her actions are lodged within a cultural practice, presumably their wrongfulness is lodged there as well. In Kargar's case, for example, there was no wrongfulness associated with his physical movements because his actions were culturally benign.

The same does not hold for Kimura, however, for her actions were not considered benign within her own culture. But how should the state properly assess the degree of Kimura's criminal responsibility? By posing this question, we are returning to the theoretical issue of whether the right to cultural autonomy should be understood to entail an obligation of cultural deference by American criminal courts. Concerns about Kimura's criminal responsibility seem to require such deference because the wrongfulness of her conduct can only be measured by the Japanese community that now (we can suppose) assigns blame for acts of *oya-ko-shinju* by virtue of the fact that they are no longer sanctioned by (endorsed and enforced by) the norm circle that once sanctioned them.

To measure Kimura by American standards of blameworthiness, however, is something of a category mistake because Americans have no cultural standard of measure against which to evaluate her actions. Her actions, in other words, are normatively evaluable only within the context of her own culture. If the right to cultural autonomy requires cultural outsiders to recognize and respect this point, then it might seem also to entail an obligation for American courts to identify and follow the blameworthy judgments of a defendant's native culture.

Interestingly, the Japanese-American community in Los Angeles rallied to Kimura's side during the litigation and submitted a petition on her behalf. The petition, signed by over twenty-five thousand people, claimed that in Japan Kimura's actions would be treated much as involuntary manslaughter is treated in California, and suggested that her sentence would be rather light (Woo, 1989, p. 404). (Curiously, Kimura's actual sentence of one year in jail and five years' probation approximates the type of sentence she would likely receive in Japan, according to the petition (Chiu, 2006, p. 1350).) While petitions of this sort have no legal standing in the courts, in Kimura's case the petition presented by the Japanese-American community fortunately provided the kind of information necessary in order to assess her blameworthiness. Thus there is reason to conclude that in this case the punishment did in fact fit the crime.

However, this outcome seems to be more of a happy coincidence than sound jurisprudence. Such an outcome might be more likely in Category 3 cases if courts were required to consider blameworthiness in the proper cultural context, or in effect defer to cultural information of the sort presented to the California court in *Kimura* by the Japanese community of Los Angeles. But the right to cultural autonomy, as this notion is developed above, does not require such cultural deference on the part of American criminal courts. The right, once again, protects the right of cultural minorities or satellite communities to live by the norms and ideals that matter to them. This right can be honored by requiring American criminal courts to inquire into a defendant's blameworthiness as measured against her or his own community standards. The reason for making such an inquiry depends upon the need to assess blameworthiness in circumstances such as those on display in *Kimura*. This can be determined only by recourse to cultural meanings. But the failure to pursue this judicial avenue does not violate the right to cultural autonomy because this would not constitute a majority culture intrusion into the internal affairs of some minority or satellite community.

Cultural variables and the cultural defense

People v. Kimura is an intriguing case because it illustrates a situation in which minority cultural variables are relevant to the process of reaching a judgment about Kimura's blameworthiness, but they do not fit neatly into either the excuse or justification prong of traditional criminal defense. The variables do not qualify as excusing conditions because they provide no indication that Kimura suffered either cognitive or volitional impairment at the time she killed her children. (Kimura's mental state at the time remains an open question.) Similarly, they do not constitute a justification because neither of the cultural communities involved would endorse nor enforce the norm(s) that Kimura elected to act upon. Her actions were wrong from the perspective of both cultural communities, but her actions were also sufficiently foreign to the cultural community responsible for judging her actions that no clear standards for the determination of blameworthiness were available there.

There is little reason to pass judgment, albeit in hindsight, on Kimura here by recommending a particular disposition of the case. The job of theoretical inquiry is only to indicate how situations like Kimura's should be approached by the criminal justice system. Cultural information that helps clarify what the defendant did, and perhaps also why she did it, is certainly germane to this process, but it does not necessarily establish the conditions of a clear defense in terms of either justification or excuse. Fumiko Kimura did do something wrong according to the standards of both Japanese and American criminal law, but what she did was meaningful, and thus understandable, only within the norm system associated with traditional Japanese beliefs. And her wrongdoing is comprehensible only against the background of the meaning of her actions. Consequently, it is a good idea for the defense to seek out such information and introduce it either during trial or at the sentencing phase. And it is a good idea for the courts to welcome the introduction of such information.

There is an ontological issue lurking beneath these comments that should be called into view. The American legal system is now reasonably comfortable with psychological assessments of human behavior, but the relevance of culture as an influence upon human conduct suggests that legal actors might also want to become more comfortable with sociological assessments of human conduct. Psychological factors have obvious effects on human conduct. But cultural factors have such an effect as well. This seems to be the lesson learned by exploring the problems produced by the *Kimura* case, and it can be further exemplified by looking at our second Category 3 case, *People v. Chen* (1989). The issue raised by *Chen* spins around whether the court in this case made effective or adequate use of the cultural desiderata introduced by defense as an excusing condition.

On September 7, 1987, Dong Lu Chen killed his wife, Jian Wan Chen, by hitting her in the head eight times with a hammer (Gallin, 1994, p. 730). The Chen family immigrated to the US from China in 1986. On August 25, 1987, Chen confronted his wife and accused her of having an affair, and Jian Wan Chen indicated at that time that she was seeing another man. When on September 7, Chen again confronted his wife, she repeated the information about her affair, and at this point he grabbed the hammer and bludgeoned Jian Wan Chen to death (Volpp, 1994, p. 65). Following information about the social implications of a wife's infidelity upon a husband's reputation in China, introduced at trial by an expert witness for the defense, the judge in the case found Chen guilty of second degree manslaughter, a crime that in New York involves causing the death of another through recklessness (Kim, 2006, p. 207). Accordingly, Chen received an apparently rather light sentence of five years' probation.

Chen resembles *Kimura* in the superficial sense that both cases involve the use by defense of cultural data intended to demonstrate diminished capacity. What is remarkable about *Chen*, however, is that the cultural data employed by the defense led the judge to conclude that Chen's capacity was diminished well beyond what might seem reasonable or appropriate given the brutality of his actions. The anthropologist whom the defense used for its expert testimony on Chinese culture offered some general observations on how a wife's infidelity is regarded in China. He claimed that a wife's adultery "stains" a husband's honor, reflects poorly both upon himself and his family, and indicates that he has a weak character (Kim, 1997, p. 120; Kim, 2006, p. 207). He further offered his opinion that a Chinese man would react more violently to such a situation than an American (Volpp, 1994, p. 66). Whether this opinion has any scholarly or scientific merit is another matter altogether, of course, and stated in these bold terms one might entertain plausible suspicions on this score.

Largely as a result of this testimony, the judge found that Chen had become so enraged by the news of his wife's infidelity that he was unable to formulate the intent to kill that was required in order to convict him of first degree manslaughter. The judge would later indicate in a *New York Times* (1989) piece that Chen had become "temporarily, totally deranged" as a result of Jian Wan Chen's admission of infidelity (Woo, 1989, p. 422). He believed this state of mental incapacity was the result of cultural beliefs about the dishonor a husband suffers as a result of such infidelity coupled (apparently) with the cultural inclination of Chinese husbands to react violently under these circumstances. The judge characterized Chen as "the product of his culture," and described the cultural influence as "something that made him crack more easily" (Woo, 1989, p. 422).

An appreciation for the mental component of a criminal act is recognized in American law as vital to a determination of the gravity of the wrong done. A person thrown into a fit of rage by virtue of some mistreatment or maltreatment by another, and who strikes out at the offending party in an emotional outburst, is not typically considered to be as blameworthy as someone who deliberately strikes out at another in order to profit from the harm caused. People sometimes react passionately and emotionally, and thus unthinkingly, to highly disturbing or shocking events, and we appreciate that the resultant loss of control is often the result of one's emotions getting the better of one—something that seems less blameworthy than doing wrong deliberately and in spite of the fact that one can be presumed to know better. This is the point behind the presumption, built into the criminal law, that diminished capacity mitigates criminal responsibility. Someone who succumbs to the force of emotion is no longer fully functional as a responsible agent, and consequently, this person seems less culpable than the person who does wrong in a deliberate and calculating way.

In one sense, cultural data are always behind such diminished capacity. Someone driven into emotional rage by the actions of another is presumably responding to the cultural meaning of what this other person has done. Spousal infidelity can be a source of great emotional distress, for example, only in cultures where the social expectation is spousal fidelity; a culture that lacked norms for the endorsement and enforcement of spousal fidelity would likely not have to deal with problems caused by the emotional outbursts of a person who has learned that her or his spouse has been unfaithful. But it is also easy to exaggerate and misunderstand the role culture plays in such outbursts, and it looks as if this might have happened in the *Chen* decision.

The judge's 1989 explanation of his decision points in this direction (Woo, 1989, p. 422). First, the judge saw Chen as a product of his culture, which we can take to mean that Chen would react to some situation in the way deemed typical or commonplace within the culture to which he belonged. Expert testimony persuaded the judge that Chinese men are prone to react violently (because emotionally overwhelmed) if they learn of a wife's infidelity. This testimony also persuaded the judge that the social support system that would keep Chen from killing his wife, a support system that would be available in China, was missing from Chen's life in New York (Volpp, 1994. p. 73). Therefore, Chen's cultural background was "something that made him crack more easily" (Woo, 1989, p. 422) or something that "made him more susceptible to cracking under the circumstances" (Woo, 1989, p. 423).

The judge concluded a bit more than this, however, for he supposed that Chen did in fact "crack" and become "temporarily, totally deranged." Missing, however, is actual evidence of Chen's derangement, and such derangement cannot be inferred from the obvious truism that Chen was a "product of his culture." What does follow, of course, is that we would expect Chen to be upset and perhaps angered by the knowledge of Jian Wan Chen's infidelity. The result could be that he cracked, in the sense offered by the judge, or it could be that he deliberately struck out at his wife in the heat of passion. The latter possibility, in New York, would warrant a finding of first degree manslaughter (Kim, 1997, p. 121). Consequently, in the absence of any psychological evidence indicating that the news of his wife's infidelity caused total derangement, there is no reason to conclude that he did "crack." Of course, there is no reason to conclude that he did not "crack" either, and so the judge may have been right about this. Our point, however, is simply that the cultural data introduced by the defense's expert witness cannot support a conclusion in either direction, although the judge apparently supposed that it did.

In evaluating this case, we might start with the obvious: this is not a Category 1 case because Chinese culture does not appear to endorse or enforce a norm that permits a husband to kill his wife in the event she admits to marital infidelity. In fact, it seems apparent from the facts of the case that Chinese men are not to do this. They are prevented from doing so by the support system around them, as the judge acknowledged. This means that Chinese culture endorses and enforces norms *against* a husband killing an unfaithful wife. It follows that if Chen really was a product of his culture, he should have known that his anger might incline him to want to kill his wife but that he should not do so. The time frame in the case also makes Chen's actions look more vicious and vengeful than deranged; roughly two weeks passed from the time Chen first learned of his wife's infidelity to the time that he purportedly cracked.

These comments suggest a difference of some importance between *Kimura* and *Chen*. Fumiko Kimura's actions were informed by a commitment to a cultural practice that was no longer current in her cultural community; Chen, however, did not act upon a previously sanctioned cultural norm. Instead, he acted specifically against his cultural norms by killing his wife when he should have known this was not permitted by his culture. So, a diminished capacity defense is about all his attorney could rely upon, but there is room to question whether the cultural data introduced for this purpose should be considered compelling, as the judge presumed them to be.

Cultural data may well be relevant to the determination of the mental state of a defendant from some minority culture, just as they are relevant to similar determinations made with regard to defendants holding norms or norm systems that are endorsed and enforced by a majority of Americans. By allowing a diminished capacity defense in criminal jurisprudence, then, the principles of American criminal law actually require the admission of cultural data when and where they are relevant to the determination of a defendant's mental state at the time of her or his criminal wrongdoing. But if it is appropriate to use cultural data to explain why a minority defendant might suffer from some diminished capacity, it is also important to use these data wisely and not exaggerate their effect on the cognitive abilities of the defendant.

We think *Chen* illustrates the kind of missteps that may occur if cultural data are not used properly in a criminal proceeding. Given the information available, it is difficult pinpoint the precise problem with the judge's reasoning in *Chen*. It could be that the judge accepted a crude form of cultural determinism, at least with regard to non-majority cultures, and thought the defense's expert witness claimed that Chinese men invariably "crack" when their wives are unfaithful; or it could be that he simply missed the logical difference between saying that Chen's culture made him susceptible to "cracking" and saying that Chen's culture made him "crack." We have noticed already that cultural factors are frequently, if not necessarily, behind emotional responses to social events. But while learning about a spouse's infidelity would likely generate anger (along with other possible emotions), both in Chinese and American cultural communities (where fidelity norms are endorsed and enforced), it does not necessarily cause one to "crack."

Nor is the familiar reasonable person test very helpful at this point. One cannot ask if a reasonable husband, or even a reasonable Chinese husband would "crack" or lose all volitional ability under such circumstances, for losing all volitional ability is not a response to events based in any way upon reason. Perhaps we could avoid this problem by asking whether the normal or average husband, or the normal or average Chinese husband, would lose all volitional control in such circumstances. As it happens, no evidence was introduced in *Chen* to indicate that Chinese husbands typically or habitually kill their wives when they learn of spousal infidelity; in fact, the expert witness that so influenced the judge was unable to recall an incident in China where a husband did kill his unfaithful wife. But even so, such a line of argument would require for support a substantial amount of sociological and/or anthropological data in order to succeed.

Finally, there is reason to ask whether anger expressed by Chinese husbands upon learning of spousal infidelity is more ritualistic than genuinely emotional. Because of the dishonor associated with spousal infidelity, the Chinese may have developed a ritual practice around such situations—a husband displays his rage at the insult by threatening to kill his wife, and family and friends intervene to prevent him from doing so. If this plays out as ritual, the husband should understand that, rage aside, he ought not kill his wife. This is simply further reason to question whether Chen's cracking, if he did in fact crack, can be directly attributed to cultural influences that would then produce an excusing condition that should be acknowledged by American law.

Cultural meanings and criminal wrongdoing

Chen, like *Kimura*, illustrates the important role cultural information can play in the process of doing justice in criminal cases involving minority defendants, but again like *Kimura*, it also signals the challenges and difficulties associated with the effective use of cultural information in criminal proceedings. Given the established presence of various cultural minorities in the United States, it is no doubt important for the criminal justice system to develop a more sophisticated understanding of, and appreciation for, the way cultural variables influence action and affect behavior. Rather than ignore cultural difference, American criminal justice would be better served by becoming more attuned to it and incorporating it more effectively within criminal proceedings. By way of further illustration of, and elaboration upon this point, we turn to the third of our Category 3 cases: *People v. Helen Wu* (1991).

This case, also much discussed in the cultural defense literature, begins when Helen Wu killed her son, Sidney, and attempted to kill herself in what appears to be another failed parent-child suicide attempt. Helen was apparently prompted to engage in this practice upon learning from her son that his father, Gary, treated him badly and that Gary was having an affair with another woman. Helen was convicted in a California Superior Court of second degree murder and sentenced to a term of 15 years to life (Volpp, 1994, p. 84). She appealed her conviction to the California Court of Appeals claiming reversible error because the trial judge did not allow a jury instruction that included the permissibility of considering Wu's cultural background in the process of deciding upon her state of mind at the time she killed her son and attempted to take her own life (Kim, 1997, p. 128). The Court of Appeals reversed, indicating that the trial judge should have informed the jury of the permissibility of considering cultural factors when there is reason to think they are relevant to an assessment of a defendant's mental state pertinent to a finding of first or second degree murder or first degree manslaughter (Volpp, 1994, p. 86).

To appreciate the challenges posed by this case, it is necessary to call to mind some important background information. Helen Wu, a native of China, met Gary Wu in 1963 shortly before Gary immigrated to the US. In the late 1970s, Gary contacted Helen, still living in Asia, and discussed her immigration to the US and possibly having his child. In 1979 Helen did come to the US and soon afterwards gave birth to Gary's son Sidney. Shortly thereafter, Helen apparently became quite depressed because Gary showed no signs of wishing to marry her and because she had neither friends nor a social support system in the US.

She decided to return to Macau, where she had been living, and left her child with Gary. Then in 1989 Helen again returned to the US and this time she married Gary. Shortly after the marriage, Sidney told his mother about his father's abuse and his connection with another woman. Apparently distraught upon receiving this news, she decided she wanted to die, and proceeded to strangle her son to death as prelude to taking her own life (Volpp, 1994, p. 86).

At trial, the prosecution argued that Helen killed Sidney because she was angry with Gary. The defense, however, argued that her actions were the result of emotional distress at the news regarding Gary's behavior coupled with cultural views about suicide and her motherly responsibilities to her child (Kim, 1997, p. 127). The jury found her act of killing Sidney to involve intent and maliciousness, though not premeditation, and therefore returned a verdict of second degree murder according to California law. Helen's defense, however, involved a claim of diminished capacity; the emotional distress she suffered indicated that she had killed Sidney in the heat of passion, and this would mean that Helen should be convicted of first degree manslaughter under California law because the element of maliciousness was missing from her actions.

The circumstances surrounding *Wu* are curiously reminiscent of both *Kimura* and *Chen*. In all three cases, the defense relied heavily on cultural data in order to demonstrate the diminished mental capacity of the defendant, and this strategy proved generally successful in each case. And perhaps it would not be an overly great exaggeration to say that this use of cultural data in criminal defense is fairly typical of Category 3 cases, at least when a question of homicide is involved. But both *Kimura* and *Wu* differ from *Chen* on one important issue. Both *Kimura* and *Wu* involve actions undertaken by the defendant that are connected to social practice, even if the respective practices are no longer current in their respective cultures. In *Wu*, for example, the expert testimony of a transcultural psychologist indicated that Helen Wu's actions were understandable given her cultural background, though there was no indication that her cultural community would think she had acted properly according to acknowledged social norms and accepted social practice.

Unlike Kimura, however, Helen Wu lacked the supportive input of a Chinese-American community at the trial process to help shape the cultural dimension of her actions. Still, it is important to ask whether Helen Wu's recourse to parent-child suicide in response to her problems with Gary suggest diminished cognitive or volitional ability. Her actions indicate that she well understood what she was doing, and information about her cultural background suggests that she deliberately chose to adhere to certain social norms that she apparently considered controlling under the circumstances. Like Fumiko Kimura, she might have been wrong about this—wrong within the norm system of her own culture—but she is hardly the first person to have made a tragic moral mistake of this sort.

Helen Wu may have made a decision that many Chinese women could understand and sympathize with given her circumstances, and regardless of whether Chinese culture (the actual Chinese norm circle) endorses the norms that she chose to follow. Cultural change is frequently slow and uneven; old norms often die hard. It is not easy to unlearn certain norms, suddenly rejected, that were endorsed and enforced throughout much of a person's life. Of course, Helen Wu may also have "cracked", like Chen was said to have "cracked," and if this was the case, a diminished capacity defense would have been appropriate for her. The point in need of emphasis, however, is that we cannot tell which defense strategy—cultural explanation (not justification) or excuse—is warranted from the cultural data introduced at trial alone. Yet from the standpoint of criminal defense, the choice of an appropriate and culturally accurate defense is of considerable importance.

Insofar as Wu's defense involved a claim of diminished capacity, cultural data may be relevant to this determination, but as with *Chen*, we cannot directly infer diminished capacity from the cultural data that were introduced. And as with *Kimura*, the pursuit of a diminished capacity defense may have been misguided and unwarranted, for a more appropriate defense may have been available to her. Such a defense would mirror the recommendations we presented in the discussion of *Kimura*. Wu's blameworthiness can only be derived from the cultural meaning of her actions. Therefore, these actions need to be explored within their cultural context, and this should include the effort to understand the degree of blameworthiness such actions carry with Wu's cultural community.

But *Wu* raises some other intercultural issues that may complicate matters. Helen Wu faced what even a fairly unsympathetic critic should acknowledge to be a terribly difficult and heart-wrenching situation, and she had to deal with this situation without the aid and support of family, friends, or a social support system that could appreciate what she was going through. Assuming Wu did not "crack" under the strain of her predicament—and this, we suspect, is the assumption that cultural outsiders in the US might rush to make—she had only the familiar norms of her cultural community to call upon in working through her predicament. She was otherwise alone, without friends, in a culturally strange environment. Accordingly, it seems important to appreciate that her cultural background may have mattered to her in a terribly intimate way as she wrestled with her situation in the isolation of her cultural and social estrangement. And it therefore should matter to those who are called upon to sit in judgment of her "crime," not because it offers an indication of the fact of mental impairment—this seems an unnecessarily unsympathetic judgment to make—but because it makes the choices she made far more understandable.

One of the primary reasons often advanced to defend the recognition of a cultural defense in American criminal law is that such a defense would aid in realizing the ideal of personalized justice—promoting the end of assuring that the punishment fits the crime (Note, 1986). We have not employed this argument in our defense of a cultural defense because the right to cultural autonomy that drives our account of the defense requires bystanders to acknowledge that there really is no crime present in Category 1 cases. But when we turn to Category 3 cases, there is something to be said in support of the personalized justice claim. Cultural data may be important either to make the defendant's actions understandable—something required in order to judge the defendant's blameworthiness—or to make the defendant's mental state apparent—something also necessary in order to judge the wrongfulness, and hence blameworthiness, of the defendant's actions. In either case, the use of cultural data in Category 3 cases can be subsumed within traditional criminal defense strategies without the need for some sort of independent cultural defense. Justice within the American criminal justice system is always and necessarily personalized, if we mean by this that a central element of the process involves determining the degree of criminal responsibility, if any, to properly ascribe to the defendant. This is how we assure that the punishment fits the crime.

But if cultural data are to be used in the process of determining the criminal responsibility of defendants from minority cultures, these data should be used wisely and insightfully. This will not necessarily make judging the blameworthiness present in these cases any easier. Even if we conclude that Helen Wu acted in a fashion that someone in her situation and from her own cultural community could reasonably deem proper, it is still difficult to assess accurately her criminal responsibility. If her actions were understandable within her cultural context, they are also unjustifiable even within this context. In the absence of a cultural community that could hold her properly answerable for her wrongdoing and assess the level of her criminal responsibility according to its own standards, this job falls to the various American criminal justice systems that might have to confront such cases. That is, elements of the dominant culture will sit in judgment of the actions of cultural minority defendants. By now, perhaps enough has been said to indicate that the criminal justice system of a dominant culture that is also sensitive to the way cultural variation can affect thinking about justice should want to find effective ways to draw upon cultural data when doing so. This is fundamental to personalized justice.

In the case of Fumiko Kimura, this challenge was made easier because the Japanese-American community offered its own sense of her criminal responsibility. And while American courts need not be considered bound by such information, it is nonetheless instructive. While this information was lacking in the case of Helen Wu, it still seems possible to judge her criminal responsibility in an acceptable fashion. The first information necessary for such a judgment, of course, is the cultural data that render a defendant's actions understandable. Once this information is in place and generally understood, it does not seem an overly onerous challenge to assess the element of wickedness or wrongfulness displayed by a defendant's actions. This requires, however, an awareness of the way cultural norms influence and direct personal responses to the predicaments that persons must at times face. Meaningful actions are invariably culturally embedded because they involve norm-following, and norms are culturally specific. Consequently, cultural data in Category 3 cases may be best used to help assess the judgment defendants displayed in dealing with some situation, and gauge the reasonableness of their actions, in order to understand the nature of their wrongdoing. This application of cultural data would not constitute an excuse; it would help determine what punishment is proper for a defendant by allowing the criminal process to grasp the severity of the crime involved.

Culture and justice

Culture, it seems, is both relevant to and important for the pursuit of justice in the United States. As should now be apparent, this point rings true in a variety of ways. The conception of culture operative throughout our discussion involves the politically salient norm or norm cluster of some community of persons—a norm circle, as Elder-Vass puts it—whose members endorse and enforce their norms amongst themselves. The politically salient norms at issue underlie and drive the social practices that typify what we can consider a cultural community, and they separate this community from other such communities whose norm systems will differ in politically salient and, what might seem when viewed from the outside, mysterious—perhaps even objectionable—ways.

Pluralist states are composed of a great variety of these cultural communities, and of course the fact of significant religious, cultural, and moral difference has historically been the source of great and dangerous conflict within these states (as well as between them). Such states face the substantial challenge—the challenge of politics—of charting a path between a shaky stability based upon oppression, and a chaotic condition tending toward anarchy. In the US, this path has taken us in the direction of a specific conception of social justice; it has taken us toward the endorsement and enforcement of a set of norms intended to establish a peaceful coexistence among the various cultural (religious, ideological, and moral) communities present throughout the land. The norms constitutive of this political culture promote toleration of difference, and if we are to take these norms seriously, we must commit to a political environment in which no cultural community is permitted to interfere with or impose upon the practices, ways, and beliefs of other cultural communities.

This rather general account of American politics, and the American concern for social justice, has obvious implications for the operation of the various criminal justice systems operative throughout the United States, and a central purpose of this discussion has been to make some of these implications apparent. The various legal systems in the US are charged with endorsing and enforcing certain norms of the majority culture that are singled out as needing or requiring the special support of the law (the normalcy function of law). This is both an important and appropriate legal function, but in a place where social justice matters, it is ancillary to the more basic legal job of endorsing and enforcing the norms of social justice (the justice function). To meet this latter challenge, and moderate the danger of majority tyranny generated by an overly zealous commitment to the former legal function, a system of civil liberties has been built into the country's political and legal machinery. These liberties safeguard minority cultures against domination by more powerful social groups.

We have applied these fundamental convictions of American political culture to certain problems American criminal justice systems must face by virtue of the fact of social and cultural pluralism. As a result, we have defended several basic claims about the way culture affects the American commitment to social justice. First, the toleration requirement central to the American sense of social justice indicates the need to acknowledge a right to cultural autonomy for all cultural (religious, ideological, and moral) communities present within the body politic. The recognition of this right as a fundamental civil liberty yields what can be considered a cultural defense against criminal prosecution that protects the internal affairs, ways, and practices, of these disparate communities. Since the state rarely brings criminal action against those who merely follow norms endorsed and enforced by cultural majorities, it should be apparent that this civil liberty protection will matter most to minority communities.

Second, the norms of social justice produce a political identity that gives a practical construction to what it means to be an American. These norms identify the most fundamental normative commitments Americans are asked to make, trumping the claims of religion, ideology, science, and morality. The right to cultural autonomy ends when some cultural community claims the authority, based upon its own norms, to interfere with, prosecute, sanction, or otherwise obstruct the internal ways and practices of some other community. Such actions are an indication of a failure to tolerate cultural outsiders, and the police powers of the state may properly be employed to prevent such interference with the internal affairs of others. From the standpoint of social justice, intercultural disputes are not to be resolved by the unilateral actions of one of the communities involved, regardless of whether or not it constitutes a majority of the population.

Finally, some individuals, particularly immigrants, may be culturally estranged in the sense that immigration has separated them from close association with their traditional norm circles and left them culturally isolated, surrounded by outside cultural communities that they may not understand or interact with. Sometimes persons living in such conditions may, for any number of reasons, do things considered blameworthy by both their own norm circle and the norms of more dominant norm circles that now surround them. In such cases, the right to cultural autonomy does not offer individuals any civil liberty protection against criminal prosecution because their actions are *ultra vires* even when viewed within the context of their own cultural communities. But there is still reason to be mindful of the defendant's cultural background in these cases because this information is required by the normative principles that underlie the operation of American criminal justice.

Sometimes the data supplied by attention to a defendant's cultural background will serve to support a diminished capacity defense, but we have suggested that this use of relevant cultural factors might actually be less commonplace in Category 3 cases than the actual case law in this category would indicate. At other times, cultural data may be more properly used to explain a defendant's actions and thus to make them more understandable to an audience of cultural outsiders.

An accurate grasp of what the defendant did and why he or she did it may require this cultural information, and in its absence there is no apparent way to judge the blameworthiness of a defendant's actions. In both situations, however, it is worth emphasizing that the introduction of cultural data is necessary if the courts are to do justice in cases involving minority defendants, where doing justice involves fitting the proper punishment to the crime involved. This is the sense in which it is important to appreciate that principles of American justice necessitate the introduction of cultural data at trial when a defendant from a minority culture is involved.

For some, including some critics of a so-called cultural defense, this will seem objectionable. The view to which these critics cling is that the United States has a standardized criminal justice process that employs reasonably exact, objective, and universal measures of criminal responsibility. Accordingly, it is both misguided and unjust to allow cultural variables into the mix, for the American standard of criminal responsibility is the proper measure for all persons living within the reach of American criminal jurisprudence. But cases like *Kimura* and *Wu* put the lie to this. We cannot begin to think about their criminal responsibility until we get clear on what they did; and we simply cannot get clear on this without learning a good deal about the social norms that informed their actions—that is, we cannot get clear on this without grasping the cultural context that renders their actions meaningful.

Does this mean that the introduction of cultural data in cases of this sort should be considered a type of cultural defense? This, of course, is a question that has been debated in a flurry of law review articles beginning in 1986 with the Note in the *Harvard Law Review* that first broached the subject. And perhaps it is now evident that little hangs on how this question is answered. What matters is the effective use of cultural data during criminal proceedings in order to facilitate the realization of a just outcome. Given the vicissitudes of the adversarial process, the absence of a concern for cultural variables in the curriculum of most law schools, and the general lack of familiarity with the implications of cultural diversity amongst criminal lawyers, the effective use of these data may still be some way off.

Yet cases like *Kargar*, *Moua*, *Le*, *Kimura*, *Chen*, and *Wu* indicate that criminal justice systems across the country should become somewhat more culturally aware, and less culturally blind, when their operatives confront cases involving cultural minorities and minority cultural practices. It seems rather pernicious to attempt to duck this responsibility by noting that this is America, and when in America everyone should do what Americans do, for this just presents us with an unacceptably myopic picture of America. The United States is now a widely pluralist place, and it has a system of justice, both civil and criminal, that requires its citizenry to live up to the challenges and obligations this fact produces. The enduring debate over the propriety of a cultural defense in American criminal law will have served a noble and worthwhile social purpose if it does something to facilitate this outcome.

Bibliography

Ajayi, V. (2012). Violence Against Women: The Ethics of Incorporating the Cultural Defense in Legal Narrative. Georgetown Journal of Legal Ethics. *The Georgetown Journal of Legal Ethics, 25*, 401–414.

al-Hibri, A. (1999). Is Western Patriarchal Feminism Good for Third World/Minority Women? In S. Okin (Ed.), *Is Multiculturalism Bad for Women?* (pp. 41–46). Princeton: Princeton University Press.

Archer, M. (1988). *Culture and Agency*. Cambridge: Cambridge University Press.

Archer, M. (1995). *Realist Social Theory: The Morphogenetic Approach*. Cambridge: Cambridge University Press.

Archer, M. (2003). *Structure, Agency and the Internal Conversation*. Cambridge: Cambridge University Press.

Archer, M. (2012). *The Reflexive Imperative*. Cambridge: Cambridge University Press.

Bancroft, G. (1843). *History of the United States, from the Discovery of the American Continent* (10th ed.). Boston: Little, Brown and Company.

Barry, B. (1973). *The Liberal Theory of Justice*. Oxford: The Clarendon Press.

Barry, B. (2001). *Culture and Equality*. Cambridge, MA: Harvard University Press.

Bauman, Z. (1999). *Culture as Praxis*. London: Sage Publications.

Berman, H. (1983). *Law and Revolution:The Formation of the Western Legal Tradition*. Cambridge, MA: Harvard University Press.

Bickhard, M.H. (2004). The Social Ontology of Persons. In J. Carpendale & U. Müller (Eds.), *Social Interaction and the Development of Knowledge* (pp. 111–132). Mahwah, NJ: Lawrence Erlbaum Associates, Inc.

Borofsky, R. (2008). Studying "Culture" Scientifically is an Oxynmoron: The Interesting Question Is Why People Don't Accept This. In M. Brown (Ed.), *Explaining Culture Scientifically* (pp. 275–296). Seattle, WA: University of Washington Press.

Bourdieu, P. (1990). *The Logic of Practice*. Cambridge: Polity.

Bozeman, T. (1972). Religious Liberty and the Problem of Order in Early Rhode Island. *The New England Quarterly, 49*(1), 44–65.

Braunmuhl, C. (2012). *Colonial Discourse and Gender in U.S. Criminal Courts: Cultural Defenses and Prosecutions*. New York: Routledge.

Brelvi, F.S. (1997). "News of the Weird": Specious Normativity and the Problem of the Cultural Defense. *Columbia Human Rights Law Review, 28*, 657–683.

Brockunier, S. (1940). *The Irrepressible Democrat: Roger Williams*. New York: The Ronald Press.

Brown, M. (Ed.) (2008). *Explaining Culture Scientifically* (pp. 3–16). Seattle, WA: University of Washington Press.

Brown, M. (2008). Introduction: Developing a Scientific Paradign for Understanding Culture. In M. Brown (Ed.), *Explaining Culture Scientifically* (pp. 3–16). Seattle, WA: University of Washington Press.

Carr, C. (2006). *The Liberal Polity.* New York: Palgrave Macmillan.

Carr, C. (2010). *Liberalism and Pluralism.* New York: Palgrave Macmillan.

Carpendale, J. and U. Müller (Eds.) (2004). *Social Interaction and the Development of Knowledge.* Mahwah, NJ: Lawrence Erlbaum Associates, Publishers.

Chiu, D. (1994). The Cultural Defense: Beyond Exclusion, Assimilation, and Guilty Liberalism. *California Law Review, 82,* 1053–1125.

Chiu, E. (2006). Culture as Justification, Not Excuse. *American Criminal Law Review, 43,* 1317–1374.

Choi, C. (1990). Note, Application Of A Cultural Defense In Criminal Proceedings. *UCLA Pacific Basin Law Journal, 8,* 80–90.

Christman, J. (2009). *The Politics of Persons.* Cambridge: Cambridge University Press.

City of Boerne v. Flores, 521 US 507 (1997).

Cohan, J.A. (2010). Honor Killings and the Cultural Defense. *California Western International Law Journal, 40,* 177 -252.

Cohen, M. (1940). Moral Aspects of the Criminal Law. *Yale Law Journal, 49,* 987–1026

Coleman, D. (1996). Individualizing Justice through Multiculturalism: The Liberal Dilemma. *Columbia Law Review, 96,* 1093–1167.

D'Andrade, R. (2008). Some Kinds of Causal Powers That Make Up Culture. In M. Brown (Ed.), *Explaining Culture Scientifically* (pp. 19–36). Seattle, WA: University of Washington Press.

D'hondt, S. (2010). The Cultural Defense as Courtroom Drama: The Enactment of Identity, Sameness, and Difference in Criminal Trial Discourse. *Law & Social Inquiry, 35*(1), 67–98.

Davis v. Beason, 133 U.S. 333 (1890).

Dawkins, R. (1976). *The Selfish Gene.* Oxford: Oxford University Press.

Dearth, M.H. (2011). Comment: Defending the "Indefensible": Replacing Ethnocentrism with a Native American Cultural Defense. *American Indian Law Review, 35,* 621–660.

Dennett, D. (1995). *Darwin's Dangerous Idea: Evolution and the Meanings of Life.* New York: Simon & Schuster.

Dennett, D. (2003). *Freedom Evolves.* New York: Penguin Books.

Diamond, S. (1971). The Rule of Law Versus the Order of Custom. In R. Wolff (Ed.), *The Rule of Law.* (pp. 115–144). New York: Simon & Schuster.

Dorf, M.C. (1998). God and Man in the Yale Dormitories, *Virginia Law Review, 84,* 843.

Durkheim, E. (1964). *The Rules of Sociological Method.* New York: Free Press.

Eisenberg, A. & Spinner-Halev, J. (Eds.) (2005). *Minorities within Minorities: Equality, Rights and Diversity.* Cambridge: Cambridge University Press.

Elder-Vass, D. (2010). *The Causal Power of Social Structures.* Cambridge: Cambridge University Press.

Elder-Vass, D. (2012). *The Reality of Social Construction.* Cambridge: Cambridge University Press.

Elshtain, J. (2008). *Sovereignty.* New York: Basic Books.

Elster, J. (1989). *The Cement of Society.* Cambridge: Cambridge University Press.

Elster, J. (1990). *Nuts and Bolts for the Social Sciences.* Cambridge: Cambridge University Press.

Employment Division, Department of Human Resources of Oregon v. Smith, 494 US 872 (1990).

Evans-Pritchard, D. & Renteln, A. (1994). The Interpretation and Distortion of Culture: A Hmong 'Marriage by Capture' Case in Fresno, California. *Southern California Interdisciplinary Law Journal, 4*, 1–48.

Ex Parte Crow Dog, 109 US 556 (1883).

Feinberg, J. (1984). *Harm to Others: The Moral Limits of the Criminal Law* (Vol. 1). Oxford: Oxford University Press.

Feinberg, J. (1985). *Offense to Others: The Moral Limits of the Criminal Law* (Vol. 2). Oxford: Oxford University Press.

Feinberg, J. (1986). *Harm to Self: The Moral Limits of the Criminal Law* (Vol. 3). Oxford: Oxford University Press.

Feinberg, J. (1990). *Harmless Wrongdoing: The Moral Limits of the Criminal Law* (Vol. 4). Oxford: Oxford University Press.

Flathman, R. (1987). *The Philosophy and Politics of Freedom.* Chicago: University of Chicago Press.

Flathman, R. (1980). *The Practice of Political Authority.* Chicago: University of Chicago Press.

Foblets, M. & Renteln, A. (Eds.) (2009). *Multicultural Jurisprudence: Comparative Perspectives on the Cultural Defense.* Oxford: Hart Publishing.

Friedman, L. (1973). *A History of American Law.* New York: Simon & Schuster.

Fuchs, L. (1990). *The American Kaleidoscope.* Hanover, NH: University Press of New England.

Fuller, L. (1964). *The Morality of Law.* New Haven, CT: Yale University Press.

Fuller, L. (1971). Human Interaction and the Law. In R. Wolff (Ed.), *The Rule of Law.* (pp. 177–217). New York: Simon & Schuster.

Fuss, D. (1990). *Essentially Speaking.* London: Routledge.

Gallin, A. (1994). Note: The Cultural Defense: Undermining the Policies against Domestic Violence. *Boston College Law Review 35*, 723–745.

Galston, W. (1991). *Liberal Purposes.* Cambridge: Cambridge University Press.

Galston, W. (2005). *The Practice of Liberal Pluralism.* Cambridge: Cambridge University Press.

Giddens, A. (1979). *Central Problems in Social Theory.* Berkeley: University of California Press.

Giddens, A. (1984). *The Constitution of Society.* Berkeley: University of California Press.

Gilbert, M. (1989). *On Social Facts.* Princeton, NJ: Princeton University Press.

Glazer, N. (1997). *We Are All Multiculturalists Now.* Cambridge, MA.: Harvard University Press.

Golding, M. (2002). The Cultural Defense. *Ratio Juris, 15*(2), 146–158.

Goldstein, T. (1994). Comment: Cultural Conflicts in Court: Should the American Criminal Justice System Formally Recognize a "Cultural Defense"? *Dickinson Law Review, 99*, 141–168.

Good, A. (2008). Cultural Evidence in Courts Of Law. *Journal of the Royal Anthropological Institute, 14*(s1), S47–S60.

Gordon, N.A. (2001). The Implications of Memetics for the Cultural Defense. *Duke Law Journal, 50.* 1809–1834.

Greenawalt, K. (2006). *Religion and the Constitution* (Vol. 1 Free Exercise and Fairness). Princeton, NJ: Princeton University Press.

Greenawalt, K. (2014). The Cultural Defense: Reflections in Light of the Model Penal Code and the Religious Freedom Restoration Act. In W. Kymlicka, C. Lernestedt &

M. Matravers (Eds.), *Criminal Law and Cultural Diversity* (pp. 153–176). Oxford: Oxford University Press.

Griffiths, J. (1986). What is Legal Pluralism? *Journal of Legal Pluralism and Unofficial Law, 24*(1), 1–55.

Hart, H. (1961). *The Concept of Law*. Oxford: The Clarendon Press.

Hart, H. (1973). Rawls on Liberty and Its Priority. *University of Chicago Law Review, 40*, 534–555.

Heyd, D. (1996). *Toleration: An Elusive Virtue*. Princeton, NJ: Princeton University Press.

Higham, J. (1955). *Strangers in the Land*. Rutgers, NJ: Rutgers University Press.

Hohfeld, W. (1919). *Fundamental Legal Concepts*. New Haven, CT: Yale University Press.

Hollis, M. &. Lukes, S. (Eds.) (1982). *Rationality and Relativism*. Cambridge, MA: MIT Press.

Honig, B. (1999). My Culture Made Me Do It. In S. Okin (Ed.), *Is Multiculturalism Bad for Women?* (pp. 35–40). Princeton, NJ: Princeton University Press.

Huntington, S. (1981). *American Politics: The Promise of Disharmony*. Cambridge, MA: The Belknap Press.

Huntington, S. (2004). *Who Are We? The Challenges to America's National Identity*. New York: Simon & Schuster.

James, S. (1984). Ecclesiastical Authority in the Land of Roger Williams. *The New England Quarterly, 57*(3), 323–346.

Kim, N. (1997). The Cultural Defense and the Problem of Cultural Preemption: A Framework for Analysis. *New Mexico Law Review, 27*, 101–139.

Kim, N. (2006). Blameworthiness, Intent, and Cultural Dissonance: The Unequal Treatment Of Cultural Defense Defendants. *University of Florida Journal of Law & Public Policy, 17*, 199–229.

Kingsbury, G. & Smith, G. (1915). *History of the Dakota Territory* (Vol. 2). Chicago, IL: S.J. Clarke Publishing Co.

Kukathas, C. (2003). *The Liberal Archipelago*. Oxford: Oxford University Press.

Kymlicka, W. (1995). *Multicultural Citizenship*. Oxford: The Clarendon Press.

Kymlicka, W., Lernestedt, C. & Matravers, M. (Eds.). (2014). *Criminal Law and Cultural Diversity*. Oxford: Oxford University Press.

Lacey, N. (2014). Community, Culture, and Criminalization. In W. Kymlicka, C. Lernestedt & M. Matravers (Eds.), *Criminal Law and Cultural Diversity* (pp. 47–66). Oxford: Oxford University Press.

Ladd, J. (1973). *Ethical Relativism*. Belmont, CA: Wadsworth Publishing Co.

Larmore, C. (1996). *The Morals of Modernity*. Cambridge: Cambridge University Press.

Lee, C. (2007). Cultural Convergence: Interest Convergence Theory Meets the Cultural Defense. *Arizona Law Review, 49*, 911–959.

Legarre, S. (2007). The Historical Background of the Police Power. *Journal of Constitutional Law, 9*(3), 745–796.

Lernestedt, C. (2014). Criminal Law and 'Culture.'. In W. Kymlicka, C. Lernestedt & M. Matravers (Eds.), *Criminal Law and Cultural Diversity*. (pp. 15–46). Oxford: Oxford University Press.

Levine, K. (2003). Negotiating the Boundaries of Crime and Culture: A Sociolegal Perspective on Cultural Defense Strategies. *Law and Social Inquiry, 28*(1), 39–86.

Llewellyn, K. & Adamson Hoebel, E. (1941). *The Cheyenne Way: Conflict and Case Law in Primitive Jurisprudence*. Norman, OK: University of Oklahoma Press.

Lowenherz, R. (1959). Roger Williams and the Great Quaker Debate. *American Quarterly. 11*(2), 157–165.

Lukes, S. (2008). *Moral Relativism*. New York: Picador.
MacIntyre, A. (1999). *Dependent Rational Animals*. Chicago, IL: Open Court.
Madison, J. (1961). Federalist #48. In *The Federalist Papers: Hamilton, Madison, and Jay*. New York: Mentor Books.
Magnarella, P.J. (1991). Justice in a Culturally Pluralistic Society: The Cultural Defense on Trial. *The Journal of Ethnic Studies 19*(3), 65–84.
Mendus, S. & Edwards, D. (Eds.). (1987). *On Toleration*. Oxford: The Clarendon Press.
Mill, J.S. (1951). *Utilitarianism, Liberty, and Representative Government*. New York: E.P. Dutton and Company, Inc.
Moore, L. (1963). Roger Williams and the Historians. *Church History, 32*(4), 432–451.
NAACP v. Alabama, 357 US 449 (1958).
Note. (1986). The Cultural Defense in Criminal Law. *Harvard Law Review, 99*, 1293–1311.
Nuotio, K. (2014). Between Denial and Recognition: Criminal Law and Cultural Diversity. In W. Kymlicka, C. Lernestedt & M. Matravers (Eds.), *Criminal Law and Cultural Diversity* (pp. 67–88). Oxford: Oxford University Press.
Nussbaum, M. (1999). *Sex and Social Justice*. New York: Oxford University Press.
Nussbaum, M. (2008). *Liberty of Conscience*. New York: Basic Books.
Obergefell v. Hodges, 135 S. Ct. 2598 (2015).
Okin, S. (1999). Is Multiculturalism Bad for Women? In S. Okin (Ed.), *Is Multiculturalism Bad for Women?* (pp. 9–24). Princeton, NJ: Princeton University Press.
Okin, S. (2005). Multiculturalism and Feminism: No Simple Question, No Simple Answers. In A. Eisenberg and J. Spinner-Halev (Eds.) *Minorities within Minorities: Equality, Rights and Diversity*. (pp. 67–89). Cambridge: Cambridge University Press.
Parekh, B. (2000). *Rethinking Multiculturalism: Cultural Diversity and Political Theory*. Cambridge, MA: Harvard University Press.
Parekh, B. (2014). Cultural Defense and the Criminal Law. In W. Kymlicka, C. Lernestedt & M. Matravers (Eds.), *Criminal Law and Cultural Diversity*. (pp. 104–118). Oxford: Oxford University Press.
Parrington, V. (1927). *Main Currents in American Thought*. New York: Harcourt, Brace & Co.
Phillips, A. (2007). *Multiculturalism without Culture*. Princeton, NJ: Princeton University Press.
Pitkin, H. (1988). Are Freedom and Liberty Twins? *Political Theory, 16*(4), 523–552.
Preyer, K. (1982). Penal Measures in the American Colonies: An Overview. *The American Journal of Legal History 26*(4), 326–353.
Quinton, A. (Ed.) (1967). *Political Philosophy*. Oxford: Oxford University Press.
Rawls, J. (1958). Justice as Fairness. *Philosophical Review, 67*(2), 164–194.
Rawls, J. (1971). *A Theory of Justice*. Cambridge, MA: Harvard University Press.
Rawls, J. (1993). *Political Liberalism*. New York: Columbia University Press.
Raz, J. (1979). *The Authority of Law*. Oxford: The Clarendon Press.
Renteln, A. (1993). A Justification of the Cultural Defense as Partial Excuse. *Southern California Review of Law and Women Studies, 7*, 437–526.
Renteln, A. (2004). *The Cultural Defense*. Oxford: Oxford University Press.
Renteln, A. (2014). What Do We Have to Fear from the Cultural Defense? In W. Kymlicka, C. Lernestedt & M. Matravers (Eds.), *Criminal Law and Cultural Diversity*. (pp. 177–204). Oxford: Oxford University Press.
Reynolds v. US, 98 U.S. 145 (1879).
Rosenmeier, J. (1968). The Teacher and the Witness: John Cotton and Roger Williams. *The William and Mary Quarterly, 25*(3), 408–431.

Sacks, V.L. (1996). An Indefensible Defense: On the Misuse of Culture in Criminal Law. *Arizona Journal of International and Comparative law 13*, 523–549.

Schapera, I. (1972). Some Anthropological Concepts of "Crime": The Hobhouse Memorial Lecture. *The British Journal of Sociology, 23*(4), 381–394.

Schatzki, T. (1996). *Social Practices.* Cambridge: Cambridge University Press.

Schatzki, T. (2002). *The Site of the Social.* University Park, PA: Pennsylvania State University Press.

Searle, J. (1969). *Speech Acts: An Essay in the Philosophy of Language.* Cambridge: Cambridge University Press.

Searle, J. (1995). *The Construction of Social Reality.* New York: Free Press.

Searle, J. (2010). *Making the Social World.* Oxford: Oxford University Press.

Sewell Jr. (1992). A Theory of Structure: Duality, Agency, and Transformation. *American Journal of Sociology, 98*(1), 1–29.

Shachar, A. (2014). Family Matters: Is There Room for 'Culture' in the Courtroom? In W. Kymlicka, C. Lernestedt & M. Matravers (Eds.), *Criminal Law and Cultural Diversity* (pp. 119–152). Oxford: Oxford University Press.

Sharafi, M. (2008). Justice in Many Rooms Since Galanter: De-Romanticizing Legal Pluralism Through the Cultural Defense. *Law and Contemporary Problems, 71*, 139–146.

Sherbert v. Verner, 374 U.S. 398 (1963).

Shklar, J. (1997). *American Citizenship.* Cambridge, MA: Harvard University Press.

Sing, J.J. (1999). Note. Culture as Sameness: Toward a Synthetic View of Provocation and Culture in the Criminal Law. *Yale Law Journal. 108*, 1845–1884.

Smith, R. (1997). *Civic Ideals.* New Haven, CT: Yale University Press.

Song, S. (2007). Justice, Gender, and the Politics of Multiculturalism. Cambridge: Cambridge University Press.

Spinner, J. (1994). *The Boundaries of Citizenship.* Baltimore, MD: Johns Hopkins University Press.

Spinner-Halev, J. (2000). *Surviving Diversity: Religion and Democratic Citizenship.* Baltimore, MD: Johns Hopkins University Press.

Starrett, G. (2008). When Theory Is Data: Coming to Terms with 'Culture' as a Way of Life. In M. Brown (Ed.), *Explaining Culture Scientifically* (pp. 253–274). Seattle, WA: University of Washington Press.

State v. Butler, C-85-05-32135 (Circuit Court of the State of Oregon for the County of Multnomah 1985).

State v. Kargar, 679 A.2d 81 (Me. 1996).

Stead, G. (1934). Roger Williams and Massachusetts-Bay. *New England Quarterly, 7*(2), 235–257.

Suri, S. (2000). A Matter of Principle and Consistency: Understanding the Battered Woman and Cultural Defenses. *Michigan Journal of Gender & Law. 7*, 107–139.

Taylor, T. (1997). Note: The Cultural Defense and its Irrelevancy in Child Protection Law. *Boston College Third World Law Journal.* 17, 331–364.

Tribe, L. (1978). *American Constitutional Law.* Mineola, NY: The Foundation Press, Inc.

The People v. Assad, 189 Cal. App. 4th 187 (Cal Ct. App. 2010).

The People v. Chen, 87-7774 (N.Y. Sup. Ct. 1998).

The People v. Kimura, A-091133 (Santa Monica Super. Ct. 1985).

The People v. Moua, 315972-0 (Fresno Super. Ct. 1985).

The People v. Wu (1991).

Tushnet, M. (1988). *Red, White, and Blue.* Cambridge, MA: Harvard University Press.

United States v. Le, 2009 U.S. Dist. LEXIS 83933 (US District Ct. ED VA 2009).

United States v. Lee, 455 U.S. 252 (1982).

Volpp, L. (1994). (Mis)Identifying Culture: Asian Women And The "Cultural Defense". *Harvard Women's Law Journal, 17*, 57–101.

Volpp, L. (1996). Talking "Culture": Gender, Race, Nation, and the Politics of Multiculturalism. *Columbia Law Review, 96*, 1573–1617.

Waldron, J. (2002). One Law for All? The Logic of Cultural Accommodation. *Washington & Lee Law Review, 59*, 3–34.

Walzer, M. (1996). *What it Means to be an American*. New York: Marsilio Publishers.

Wanderer, N. &. Connors, C.R. (1999). Culture and Crime: Kargar and the Existing Framework for a Cultural Defense. *Buffalo Law Review, 47*, 829–873.

Warnock, M. (1987). The Limits of Toleration. In Mendus, S. & Edwards, D. (Eds.) *On Toleration*. Oxford: Clarendon Press.

Williams, B. (1996). Toleration: An Impossible Virtue? In D. Heyd (Ed.), *Toleration: An Elusive Virtue*. Princeton, NJ: Princeton University Press.

Williams, B. (2005). *In the Beginning Was the Deed*. Princeton, NJ: Princeton University Press.

Winch, P. (1967). Authority. In A. Quinton (Ed.). *Political Philosophy*. (pp. 97–111). Oxford: Oxford University Press.

Winch, P. (1972). *Ethics and Action*. London: Routledge & Kegan Paul.

Wisconsin v. Yoder, 406 U.S. 205 (1972).

Wittgenstein, L. (1958). *Philosophical Investigations* (2nd ed.). New York: Macmillan.

Wolff, R. (Ed.). (1971). *The Rule of Law*. New York: Simon & Schuster.

Wolff, R. (1977). *Understanding Rawls*. Princeton, NJ: Princeton University Press.

Woo, D. (1989). The People v. Fumiko Kimura: But Which People? *International Journal of the Sociology of Law, 17*, 403–428.

Zakai, A. (1991). Orthodoxy in England and New England: Puritans and the Issue of Religious Toleration, 1640–1650. *Proceedings of the American Philosophical Society, 135*(3), 401–441.

Index

For Product Safety Concerns and Information please contact our EU representative GPSR@taylorandfrancis.com Taylor & Francis Verlag GmbH, Kaufingerstraße 24, 80331 München, Germany

Batch number: 10725973

Printed by Printforce, the Netherlands